COOKBOOK

TORMONT

COOKBOOK

CONTENTS

Introduced by Felicity Salter
Photographed by Peter Barry
Recipes styled by Helen Burdett
Designed by Alison Jewell and Sally Strugnell
Jacket Design by Zapp
Edited by Jillian Stewart

Published in 1992 by Tormont Publications Inc.
338 Saint Antoine St. East, Montreal, Canada   H2Y 1A3
Tel. (514) 954-1441   Fax (514) 954-1443

Printed in Canada
ISBN 2-89429-123-X

What is healthy eating?

It seems that for every authority that tells you to eat more of some food, another tells you not to bother…fat is bad, eat oily fish, cut down on sugar, eat dried apricots, bananas are bad for you, don't eat bread, eat baked potatoes, etc., etc. Clearly, as the awareness of healthy eating increases, it also becomes harder to sort out all the advice and differing opinions.

The importance of exercise

Although this book is particularly concerned with sensible eating, it is important to remember that health, diet and fitness are all linked. No matter how conscientious you are with your food, you'll also need to take regular exercise. It's best to aim to exercise at least 2 or 3 times a week for approximately 30 minutes each time. Take things gradually though, if you haven't exercised for some time. Start by trying to walk on a frequent basis rather than taking the car. Make the effort to walk up stairs rather than being lazy and always opting for the elevator. When you become more fit you can then try running up the stairs. Once you have mastered that, try and join a gym or class and make exercise a natural part of your life. You may like to take up jogging – but seek your doctor's approval before starting. Keeping fit by taking regular exercise not only makes you feel better, but you'll find that you actually have more energy too. It will also mean that your metabolic rate – that is basically the rate at which your body uses food – will increase. So you'll tend not to store fat, but use it.

Of course, there are other factors affecting

Regular exercise is very beneficial.

health apart from diet and exercise, such as heredity, illnesses and smoking. There is little point eating and exercising conscientiously if you are still smoking – so give up! Taking care of your health through diet and exercise isn't just a case of adding a few more years onto your life span, one in 3 deaths in people over 35 could be postponed by making changes to the diet, and far more people would enjoy an active and healthy life well into old age, if they lived a healthier lifestyle.

Variety is the key to a healthy diet.

A balanced diet explained

The belief in the value of a balanced diet grew out of the realization that if a large enough variety of foods were consumed, this would prevent deficiencies in any nutrients. Ironically, it is our lack of ability to choose our foods sensibly from the enormous range available, that has helped to cause some of today's health problems:

• Heart disease kills about 770,000 people in the U.S. each year

• About 20% of all Americans are clinically overweight or obese.

So if variety is the key to good health, it is essential to understand the elements which contribute to a healthy eating plan.

No single food can provide adequate amounts of all protein, fats, carbohydrates, vitamins and minerals necessary to maintain health and vitality. Therefore it is crucial to choose a variety of foods that not only taste good, but also provide the right balance of nutrients. It is the 'balance' and the selection and combination of foods chosen which will help you to avoid eating too much of some foods, while ensuring that the nutrients you require are then consumed in adequate amounts.

The following chart explains what the essential nutrients are, in which foods they may be found and their role in the body. The U.S. Senate Select Committee on Nutrition and Human Needs made a number of recommendations

NUTRIENT	IMPORTANT SOURCES OF NUTRIENT	SOME MAJOR FUNCTIONS	
		BUILDING & MAINTENANCE	REGULATORY PROCESSES
PROTEIN	Meat, poultry, fish, legumes, eggs, cheese, milk, nuts.	Promotes growth and repair of tissues. Forms structure of every cell, such as muscle, blood, bone, skin, hair, nails. Maintains healthy body cells.	Makes up part of enzymes, some hormones and body fluids and the antibodies which increase resistance to infection.
CARBOHYDRATE	Bread, cereal, sugar, potatoes, beans.	Supplies energy and can be used for growth and maintenance of body cells.	Unrefined products supply fiber to promote regular bowel movement.
FAT	Butter, margarine, oil, milk, cheese, fatty meats.	Most concentrated source of energy. Constitutes part of structure of every cell. Supplies essential fatty acids.	Provides and carries fat-soluble vitamins A, D, E and K.
VITAMINS	Fresh fruit and vegetables, dairy products, nuts, liver, kidney.	Increases resistance to infection. Strengthens blood vessels, healing wounds and bones.	Regulates metabolic processes.
MINERALS CALCIUM	Milk, yogurt, bread, cheese, cereals, sardines, canned salmon (with bones), green vegetables, citrus fruits, legumes.	Combines with other minerals to give structure and strength to bones and teeth.	
IRON	Liver, kidneys, red meat, bread, potatoes, egg yolk, green vegetables, legumes, cereals.	Combines with protein to form hemoglobin, the red substance in blood that carries oxygen and carbon dioxide to the cells.	Functions as part of enzymes in tissue respiration.
SODIUM	Salt, salt found in foods such as bacon, ham, smoked fish, cheese, butter, margarine and most other processed food.		Maintains water balance in the body.
POTASSIUM	Milk, fruit juice, bananas, dried fruits, meat, bran, peanut butter, legumes, potatoes.	Helps release of energy from carbohydrates, proteins and fats.	Required for muscle contraction.
MAGNESIUM	Green vegetables (raw), nuts especially almonds and cashews, soya beans, seeds, whole grains.	Building bones and manufacturing proteins.	Helps functioning of nerves.
PHOSPHORUS	Milk, cheese, yogurt, wholemeal bread other cereals, malt, fish, eggs, vegetables.	Maintains healthy bones. Important for energy release.	
ZINC	Meat, liver, eggs, poultry, seafood, milk, whole grains.	Growth and synthesis of proteins, wound healing, aids sexual maturation. Maintenance of hair, nails and mucous membranes.	Required for normal functioning of thyroid gland.
IODINE	Seafood, iodized salt, sea salt.		Essential for maintaining normal metabolism in all the body's cells.
FLUORINE	Fish, tea, drinking water.	Formation of healthy bones and teeth and resistance to dental decay.	

after looking at the average American diet. They advised that fat intakes should be reduced to provide no more than 30% of our total energy intake, a significant reduction from the national average of 40%. Saturated (animal fats) should also be reduced. The American Heart Association and the National Research Council committee on diet and cancer made the same recommendation.

The same groups recommended that sugar and salt consumption be reduced, but advised Americans to eat more fiber.

No recommendations either to increase or decrease total protein intake have been made. Other recommendations, would however, ensure a greater proportion of protein being consumed from vegetable sources.

The energy content of the diet should be sufficient for individuals to maintain optimum body weight and allow adequate exercise.

There were also recommendations to moderate alcohol consumption and not to smoke.

Looking back

Many years ago man hunted for food, feasted, then spent several days searching for the next meal. Fat was invaluable then, as it was stored to provide a reserve source of energy. Today, however, food is abundant and we don't go for days without eating – therefore our reserve fat store remains. We are also generally less active than our predecessors – so as a result fat is stored and builds up to become excess weight. Most of us eat too much fat and because it provides more energy (calories) weight for weight, than other foods, it is often one of the major causes of obesity. In fact, it is not just a case of how much fat we eat, we should also be concerned with the sort of fat.

What are the different types of fat in food?

The most common form of fat, making up approximately 98% of that present in the body, is termed neutral fat, or triglycerides. These fats, or triglycerides are made up of fatty acids and glycerol in a ratio 3:1 respectively. Usually a proportion of each of the three basic categories of fatty acids, (saturated, mono-unsaturated and polyunsaturated) exist but one type of fatty acid predominates. The type of fat will depend on the relative quantities of these fatty acids and will then be classified as saturated, mono-unsaturated or polyunsaturated.

Saturated fats

These contain a majority of saturated fatty acids, or saturates and are usually solid at room temperature. Foods rich in saturated fat are nearly always of animal origin. The exceptions to this are coconut and palm oil. Butter, lard, cream, whole milk, cheese, suet and visible meat fats are typical, but margarine and hydrogenated vegetables oils are also examples of saturated fats. Saturated fats can increase blood cholesterol level, and for those susceptible, this in turn can be a contributory factor in heart disease.

Polyunsaturated fats

These are rich in polyunsaturated acids and are generally liquid or very soft at room temperature and when refrigerated. They are usually of vegetable origin, although fish oils break this rule, being high in polyunsaturated fatty acids.

The main sources of polyunsaturated fat include: corn, safflower, sunflower, peanut and canola oils, and polyunsaturated margarine. Polyunsaturated fats can lower the blood cholesterol level.

Mono-unsaturated fats

These contain fatty acids which are mainly mono-unsaturated in nature. They are soft or liquid at room temperature, but may solidify in cold temperatures. The most well known source is olive oil, but it is also present in the fat of poultry and oily fish such as mackerel, herring and salmon.

So to clarify, it is important to understand that no single food contains only one sort of fat; it is the proportion to which varying fats are present, which distinguishes the different foods.

Shortening, for example,

contains ten times as much saturated fat as it does polyunsaturated, whereas, whole wheat bread has twice as much polyunsaturated fat as saturated.

A note about margarines

Some people are under the misconception that margarines are better for you than butter, although this may often not be the case.

Several margarine manufacturers start with cheap ingredients such as beef suet or whale oil and then rely on extensive processing, coloring or additions to produce a palatable result.

They also use a process known as hydrogenation which solidifies fat, but in turn alters unsaturated fats into saturated fats. So look for margarines made from cold pressed unsaturated oils (which have not been hydrogenated) in health food stores.

Cholesterol in Food

Meat	Mg per 100g
Brains	2200
Liver	260-43
Lean duck breast	160
Lamb, lean	110
Beef, lean	82
Chicken, breast	74
Turkey, breast	62

Dairy products	Mg per 100g
Egg yolk	1260
Egg, whole	450
Butter	230
Parmesan cheese	90
Edam cheese	72
Cheddar cheese	70
Milk, whole	14
Milk, skimmed	2
Egg white	0

Fish	Mg per 100g
Prawns	200
Fish, white	70
Fish, oily	80

Miscellaneous	
Lard	70+
Margarine (from animal fat)	65
Margarine (from vegetable fat)	0
Vegetables & cereals	0

What is cholesterol?

Cholesterol is a fat-like substance which is produced in the bodies of all animals, including man. Animal foods will therefore contain some cholesterol, whereas foods of vegetable origin contain very little, if any. Cholesterol is an important body constituent required for normal day to day functioning of the body.

Functions of cholesterol:

• Forms part of cell membranes and protects nerve fibers
• Involved in the manufacture of hormones, particularly sex hormones and those which regulate the body's digestive system

Cholesterol is a constituent of Vitamin D which is manufactured by the body from the action of sunlight on the body. But you don't need very much – every day the body manufactures approximately 1g of cholesterol and it makes a further 0.5g from the diet. The body actually produces four times more than it needs, so there is no risk of a cholesterol deficiency.

Cholesterol is transported around the body in the bloodstream and some people have a tendency to lay down an excess of cholesterol as fatty deposits in the blood vessels. If the body doesn't process this properly, it will build up year by year to such an extent that the cholesterol levels become dangerously high. The heart then has to work exceptionally hard to pump the blood through.

Since saturated fats can increase blood cholesterol, it is therefore best to keep consumption low.

Many of the so called diseases of civilization such as cancer, heart disease, high blood pressure, obesity and diverticulitis are becoming increasingly linked with high cholesterol diets.

As long ago as 1916, studies comparing the low fat diets of the Japanese to the cholesterol-rich diets of northern Europe and America, found a high correlation between high fat, low fiber, Western diets and cancer and heart disease.

However, no conclusive evidence has evolved relating dietary cholesterol to raised blood cholesterol levels. Nevertheless, a diet high in saturated fatty acids is believed to raise the blood cholesterol levels, whereas, polyunsaturated fatty acids may reduce the level.

It is believed that reducing our total fat intake, especially of saturated fat, should have long term benefits and may help to reduce the risk of ill health. Medical experts are therefore advising that we should:

• Reduce total fat in the diet
• Limit saturated fat intake to approximately ⅓ of the total fat in the diet, replacing saturated fat with polyunsaturated fat as much as possible

Why eat less fat?

Apart from the need to eat less saturated fat to reduce the risks of high blood cholesterol levels, bear in mind the following points:
• Half the fat we eat is surplus to the fat we need
• Although we need some fat in our diet for energy and to supply the essential fat soluble vitamins, we do need to reduce our intake (on average an adult needs no more than 3oz/75g of fat each day)
• Fat contains over 200 calories per 1oz (25g). Therefore, a high fat diet will certainly be high in calories and as a result will encourage weight gain
• You are what you eat, so it makes sense to eat less fat

Avoiding fats

This can be very difficult unless you make everything yourself, and although it is nice to, we don't always have the time. A surprising number of processed foods tend to contain fats, so read labels carefully, and remember that ingredients are listed in order of importance.

This leaves the fat present in natural foods. These may contain fat, but also have a high food value. Eggs for example have approximately 11% total fat content, raw, boiled or poached, yet they are also a good source of protein and vitamins.

Practical ways to cut down on fat

• Eat more meat-free meals
• When buying meat, choose lean cuts
• Trim off visible fat from all meat
• Remove skin from poultry
• Replace whole milk with skimmed (except for young children)
• Use low fat cottage cheese or natural yogurt instead of cream
• Eat fruit flavored, low fat yogurt, instead of mousses or soufflés
• Have sherbet instead of ice cream
• Have fresh fruit salads instead of cakes and pies
• Replace full fat cheese e.g. Cheddar and Swiss with medium fat cheeses, such as mozzarella, or eat low fat cheeses, such as cottage cheese
• Use low calorie salad dressings instead of mayonnaise
• Spread sandwiches with reduced calorie dressings, instead of butter
• Replace cream-filled cakes and chocolate cookies with whole grain alternatives
• Garnish baked potatoes with chives and natural yogurt instead of butter
• Instead of deep frying, shallow fry or roast without additional fat
• If shallow frying, always make

sure that the fat is thoroughly preheated, so that the fat absorbed into the food is minimized
• Boil, bake, grill and poach where possible
• Cook with non-stick pans to reduce the amount of fat needed
• Use gentle heats when using unsaturated fats, since they can change into saturated fats during cooking

What is dietary fiber?

It is a form of carbohydrate which is naturally present in foods of plant origin – that includes fruit, vegetables, legumes, cereals and seeds. It is what makes up the skeleton of plants, the husks of grains, the shells of beans and the skins of fruit and vegetables. For many years this part of foods was considered superfluous and because it often gave food a chewier texture it was often refined away e.g. brown flour was refined to produce white flour.

Fiber values are therefore often reduced by processing or refining, yet they are also reduced in cooking too. Take, for example, a fresh apple – this contains approximately 1.8g of dietary fiber to each 100g. If cooked and made into apple-sauce, this reduces dietary fiber to 1.5g per 100g. This is reduced even further when made into apple juice – when it no longer contains any fiber.

Why do we need fiber?

Fiber is made up of complex carbohydrates which cannot be

digested by the body and for this reason it was considered of no dietary value for many years.

Recent research linked insufficient fiber in the diet with a whole range of disorders, such as diverticulosis, hemorrhoids, gallstones and varicose veins, as well as conditions as serious as heart disease, diabetes and cancer of the colon. These complaints, often called diseases of affluence, are all relatively common in Western societies where diets are often low in fiber. In comparison, in developing countries, where diets are high in fiber, the same problems do not appear to occur.

How much fiber should we be eating?

Expert opinion is united in recommending that people consume more fiber. Unfortunately, in this century Americans have been eating more refined foods, which have been stripped of fiber, and more meat, which contains none.

The easiest way to eat more fiber is to eat more unrefined foods – remembering that only plant foods have fiber. The recipes in this book use a good balance of foods high in fiber, from cereals and nuts, to fruit and vegetables.

Is it possible to eat too much fiber?

Fiber in the diet should be increased gradually. Too much, too quickly, can cause stomach ache. Fiber can have a laxative effect and large amounts of insoluble fiber may cause

excessive flatulence, and an initial bloating feeling, due to the water it absorbs in the stomach. So the rule is to adapt your diet slowly, and you'll benefit in both the short and long term. For example, change to whole grain bread this week, then add a piece of fruit with skin on, each day. Introduce whole grain cereals and try making pastry, muffins etc. with ½ whole wheat flour and ½ white flour. In the next month, try adding beans and lentils to casseroles, then slowly introduce dried fruits and nuts.

Many everyday foods contain fiber.

Role of salt in the body

Salt is a naturally occuring compound made up of sodium and chloride, hence the name sodium chloride. Approximately 10% of sodium is found in tissue cells, 40% is present in bone cells and the remaining 50% is located outside the cells in the body fluids.

Sodium is needed for nerve and muscle functioning, and to

maintain the fluid balance mechanism. It is also a major factor in determining blood pressure. Chlorine plays an important part in digestion, because it is a major element in the acid present in our stomachs and like sodium, it is essential for the correct functioning of the nervous system.

The need for water and salt is closely linked. Too little salt may result in muscular cramps, whereas high salt intakes are likely to cause a feeling of thirst. Loss of fluid through perspiration results in the concentration of sodium increasing in the remaining body fluid, which consequently makes you thirsty. Salt is therefore an essential dietary requirement in small quantities.

The functions of salt

For many years man has used salt as a preservative, in cured meats for example. It is an important textural agent in many manufactured foods, and it is equally necessary in making basic foods such as bread and cheese. However, we are most familiar with its function as a flavor enhancer.

The disadvantages of salt

In theory, surplus salt should be excreted via the kidneys. In practice, some people's kidneys do this more efficiently than others. Too much salt creates extra work for the kidneys and may result in excess fluid retention. This can sometimes be seen as swelling of the face, hands or ankles, and can cause a rise in blood pressure. In those vulnerable to high blood pressure, eating too much salt leads to a higher risk of a heart attack or stroke. This link between high blood pressure and salt was established as long ago as 1928.

High Sodium Foods

bacon,
baking powder and bicarbonate of soda, bread unless homemade without salt, biscuits, butter unless unsalted, cereals for breakfast – almost all apart from oatmeal, muesli and unprocessed flaked varieties, cheese, except a few labelled low sodium or homemade cheese, convenience foods (most) chips smoked and cured fish Indian meals low fat spreads margarines, unless low salt nuts, salted e.g. peanuts olives pastry, unless made with unsalted fat salad dressings sausages pies filled with meat burgers self-raising flour shellfish smoked meats soups, canned, dried soy sauce stock cubes canned vegetables yeast extract

Low Sodium Foods

barley
beans
cream
egg yolks
fruit
honey
lentils (cooked)
mustard (dry)
nuts (unsalted)
oats
pasta
potatoes
rabbit
rice
rye
sugar
wheat
soya flour
vegetable oils
wheat germ

Avoid Processed Foods

Most of the salt we eat comes from processed foods. Canned vegetables for example, have 200 times more salt than the fresh ones. So as you can see in the list of high sodium foods, it's not just the obvious foods you have to watch. Many food additives are based on sodium. However, they are generally present in each item in relatively small proportions, so they should not be a cause for concern in themselves. It is the accumulation of many processed foods which causes a problem. Look out for the increasing range of products that are now sold optionally without salt, such as canned corn.

Manufactured foods tend to have a far higher proportion of sodium. Natural foods, by comparison, contain either roughly equal amounts of sodium and potassium, or they are higher in potassium. It is important to try and maintain the correct sodium/ potassium balance in the body, and excess salt can disrupt this.

Getting the balance right

Most of us find food without any salt bland and uninteresting. However, we tend to eat salt mainly out of habit and it is possible to adapt the taste buds in just a few weeks to want less salt.

Steps to reducing salt intake

• Limit foods containing high levels of salt
• Reduce or omit the addition of salt at the table
• Restrict the amount of salt added during cooking

If you find it difficult to reduce salt you may find it helpful to use alternative flavorings to cushion the change in taste.

Alternative Flavorings

WITH BEEF	horseradish, ginger, black pepper, French mustard
WITH CHICKEN	lemon juice, garlic, paprika, coriander, cumin
WITH LAMB	mint, rosemary, chili powder, garlic, turmeric, lemon juice

WITH PORK	orange juice, ginger, garlic, green onions
WITH FISH	black pepper, lemon juice, parsley, dill
WITH POTATOES	chives, green onions, dill, parsley, turmeric
WITH RICE	saffron, garlic, onion, coconut
WITH GREEN BEANS	lemon juice, mustard seeds
WITH PEAS	mint, parsley, onions
WITH CARROTS	orange juice, coriander, chives
WITH TOMATOES	basil, oregano, marjoram

When making your own bread without salt, overcome the bland flavor by mixing the dough with buttermilk instead of water. Add additional flavorings such as sesame seeds, roasted

Avoid sugary cakes and desserts.

sunflower seeds or caraway seeds.

You can also make your own baking powder by mixing equal parts of arrowroot, cream of tartar and potassium bicarbonate, (your pharmacist might even make this up for you).

All about sugar

There are many types of sugar available in foods, not just table sugar, which can be in the form of white, brown or icing sugar. Sugar is the term given to a group of carbohydrate substances.

Glucose - this is sometimes referred to as grape sugar, dextrose or corn syrup. It occurs naturally in many foods including grapes, corn and other fruit and vegetables.

Glucose is the basic unit of which all other sugars are composed, and to which most sugars and starches are broken down to by the body.

Fructose - this is also called fruit sugar. Sold in packets, it also exists naturally in fruit, many vegetables and honey. It is the sweetest of all common sugars.

Sucrose - this can be in the form of granulated, icing, brown and muscovado sugar. It may be obtained from sugar beet or sugar cane. Sucrose from sugar beet needs to be manufactured to remove the bitter tasting molasses.

Lactose - this is naturally present in milk.

All white sugar is refined. However, it may then be ground and colored, so sugar which is brown is not necessarily unrefined. It is believed that unrefined sugar contains small quantities of minerals. Nevertheless, they are present in such tiny amounts that they are of no significance.

This is why sugar has been omitted from the sugar-free section of the book and many of the recipes rely on natural sweetness or the addition of naturally sweet foods for flavor.

Sugar in manufactured foods

Apart from the sugar that you consciously add to foods, sugar is also contained in many manufactured foods. Approximately 75% of the sugar consumed in the U.S. is eaten in in this way.

Sugar is a food manufacturer's delight, offering tastiness, shelf-life and texture, all at low cost. Many foods that are considered savory contain sugar e.g. pickle is 30% sugar, chutney is 50%

whereas jam is 60%.

Although sales of packaged plain sugar has declined, sugar consumption as a whole has not, due to the fact that between 60-75% of the sugar we eat comes from manufactured foods. Coke for example contains 7tsps (35mL) sugar per glass. Just think how you would cringe if someone wanted that much sugar in their tea!

It is also the frequency at which these sugar-rich foods are consumed that is causing concern. It is this frequency which is believed to have the greatest effect on dental decay. If you have to indulge in sugary foods, it is preferable to confine it to the occasional treat.

How much sugar should we consume?

Excess sugar can lead to 2 main problems - firstly being overweight and secondly, dental decay.

It is currently estimated that we consume $\frac{1}{3}$ pound of sugar per day. This figure represents an estimated total consumption - that is table sugar plus sugar present in prepared food.

The ideal diet would contain no sucrose. Most health studies have recommended that sugar consumption be reduced. The easiest way is to cut down on processed foods.

Why eat less sugar?

• Refined sugar contains no nutrients, only calories (although less refined sugars contain some trace elements, they are only available in minimum amounts -

much less than the value of most foods)
• Sugar contains 100 calories per 25g or 110 per oz, so it is extremely high in 'empty' calories. These calories would be better 'spent' on foods providing minerals, vitamins and fiber
• Calories from sugar are quickly absorbed and therefore encourage weight gain
• Sugar is a principal factor in tooth decay (brushing the teeth only makes a marginal difference)
• Too much sugar increases the levels of fats (triglycerides) in the blood and particularly increases the fats which may be associated with circulatory complaints
• In some children, high sugar intake can result in hyperactivity
• Sugar is a drain on nutrients, especially B vitamins and calcium
• While sugar is high in calories, it is not satisfying. It is therefore easy to eat a lot. An average day's consumption of 5oz (120g) is 500 calories. To eat the same amount of calories in other foods, you would have to eat your way through nearly 1½lbs of peeled bananas or more than 3 lbs of apples.
• It drastically raises blood sugar levels

Does sugar give you energy?

In theory sugar does provide energy, but there is more to it than that. Whatever you eat raises your blood sugar level to some extent, and provided that glucose is released slowly during digestion, this blood sugar level is maintained. This sustains

mental and physical ability, helping to keep our emotions balanced.

When we eat unrefined high fiber carbohydrate, such as wholemeal bread, everything is fine, because it is digested slowly.

However, a concentrated supply of refined sugar is absorbed quickly, and this raises blood sugar to very high levels. In response to this, the pancreas sends insulin to lower the sugar level, causing a rapid fall, which causes another craving for sugar. So a vicious circle is set up causing bursts of energy, followed by fatigue.

Foods high in added sugars

Marmalade, jam, chocolate, candy, soft drinks, sweeteneed juice drinks, cookies especially chocolate, sweetened breakfast cereals, puddings, cakes, meringues, mousses, jellies, sweet liqueurs, pickles, chutneys, sauces, ketchup, canned fruit in syrup

Making the most of natural sugars

It may well be difficult to initially reduce sugar intake, so take things gradually as a means of making foods acceptable.

Within the low sugar section of this book the best possible use has been made of naturally sweet foods, as a means of sweetening varying foods. These include honey, and dried fruits such as apricots, currant, dates, figs, prunes and raisins. Nevertheless, although naturally sweet, they should not be eaten in excess.

In the early stages of sugar reduction, try using ³/₄ of the sugar you would normally add to drinks. You can gradually reduce these when this established new level has become normal and enjoyable.

The essential vitamins

The human body is a sophisticated machine which needs many elements to keep it running efficiently. Apart from protein, carbohydrates, fats and minerals the body also needs a good supply of vitamins.

Vitamins contribute to good health, by enabling the body to function at its best. They are responsible for growth

and repair of body tissues, for healthy skin, good vision, strong bones and good teeth.

Vitamins do not supply the body with any energy, although some vitamins allow energy to be released in the body from the food we eat every day.

Each vitamin is made up of individual chemicals which give it its particular properties. The letters denoting each vitamin represent the order in which they were discovered. Vitamin A was the first to be discovered in 1911.

There are thirteen major vitamins and these can be divided into two major groups - those which dissolve in water, and those which dissolve in fat. The water soluble vitamins are all of the B and C group. They dissolve in water, are easily lost in cooking and cannot be stored in the body. As a result, foods containing vitamins B and C must be eaten on a regular daily basis to ensure the body has a constant supply . Any which are additional to the body's requirements are simply excreted in the urine.

The fat soluble vitamins are A, D, E & K. These are stored in the liver, so that a daily intake is not essential. A good quantity of a rich sources, eaten once a week, is usually sufficient. Fat soluble vitamins are generally stable, but they can be sensitive to light. Freezing, however, does little damage to most.

Varying requirements

The amount of any vitamin required each day varies

according to age, sex, and occupation. Growing children and pregnant and breast feeding mothers all need more vitamins, along with the elderly and those recovering from illness. Other factors, such as diet and lifestyle also influence vitamin requirements.

The chemicals contained in alcohol, cigarettes, coffee, aspirins and the Pill use up much of the body's resources. So people who smoke, drink or take regular medication need to be sure that their food is rich in vitamins.

Is there any chance of not getting enough vitamins?

Clinical deficiencies in the West today are very rare. Marginal deficiencies however may lead to non specific symptoms such as; generally feeling unwell, a low resistance to infections, and possible restricted growth in children. The good news is that, with very few exceptions, eating a well balanced diet with sufficient variety and quantity should provide the correct daily requirement.

Storing, preparing and cooking fruit and vegetables

Fruit and vegetables are a particularly good source of vitamins, but to obtain maximum benefit, they must be treated with care.

Firstly, look for the freshest fruit and vegetables you can find - if possible, grow you own. Fresh produce is best eaten within a few days of purchase, since the vitamin content falls daily, especially if they are stored at room temperature. The refrigerator helps reduce the rate of vitamin lost. However, if the fruit or vegetables are not required for a few days, blanch and freeze for maximum vitamin value. It's interesting to know that frozen vegetables retain many more vitamins than the canned varieties.

Where possible eat fruit and vegetables with the skin on. Peel only when you absolutely have to. Brush the skins instead of scraping them too, since there's a wealth of nutrients in the skin.

Avoid soaking vegetables in water for long periods of time before cooking, as this causes the water soluble vitamins to leach out into the water and be lost.

Ensure that vegetables are boiled in the minimum amount of water, for a minimum amount of time, to reduce vitamin loss. Use vegetable cooking water in stocks or soups. Steaming is an effective way of cooking vegetables, since they do not come into direct contact with the water. However, steaming may take a few minutes longer than boiling.

Microwaving fruit and vegetables is an excellent cooking method. The cooking time is short, and a minimum amount of liquid is used, so the loss of vitamins is minimized.

Make sure you serve raw or cooked vegetables as soon as possible after preparation.

Counting the calories

A surprising number of the population is overweight, so it is hardly surprising that dieting is so common. Most dieters crave quick results, but is this the answer?

All about calories

We have all heard the term calories in relation to slimming, but what exactly are they?

The food we eat supplies us with the energy we need to function. Much of this energy is used up in vital body functions, such as keeping the heart beating, the lungs breathing and sustaining the other vital operations that keep the body running. Of course energy is also needed for daily activities, such as walking, talking, eating etc.

Surprisingly, 75% of the energy provided by food is used as heat for the body, and 25% is converted into 'work'.

Calories therefore, provide a useful unit to measure the potential energy content of any food, as well as the amount of energy consumed during any physical activity.

Which foods provide the most calories?

Fat, carbohydrate and protein provide the body with calories. Fat is more than twice as high in calories than either carbohydrate or protein.

Cooking oil, for example, is 100% fat. Most foods, however, are a combination of different components.

Whole grain bread is not only a good source of calories, but it also provides fiber, vitamins and other nutrients, and so is an ideal energy-giving food.

How many calories do we need?

The amount of energy consumed, and therefore the amount of calories needed, depends on age, sex and the level of activity. Obviously the more active you are, the more energy you will require.

Getting the balance right

If you take in more calories than you use, the excess is stored as body fat. If you take in less, you will lose weight, the body will start to use up fat stores.

Advantages of exercise

There are several important reasons why you should exercise when slimming:

• It makes you more aware of your body

• It increases body heat, speeding up the rate at which calories are burnt. It can also discourage eating for a few hours

• It tones muscles, and good muscle tone can do much to improve the body shape

• It enhances the self image and self confidence, so comfort eating is less appealing

Which diet?

There are so many different types of diet; from low fat, high fiber, high protein, low carbohydrate to fat-free diets.

The success of any diet (in terms of weight loss) relies on the principle that less calories should be eaten than used.

However, many people opt for crash diets where you may lose weight quickly over a short period of time, but as soon as you stop, the weight tends to creep on again. Therefore, crash dieting is never really any use, since it is only maintained for a short time.

Then there's the calorie controlled diet. While following a reduced eating plan, it is very important to eat the right foods. When calorie counting alone, it is all too easy to use the allowance on 'foods' which are in fact 'empty calories' i.e. foods with no additional nutritional value such as alcohol. Instead, you should be aiming to take in as many different nutrients as possible from a wide selection of unrefined foods.

How to eat fewer calories and still maintain weight

The successful diet is one that maintains a healthy eating plan. This should be one where you don't feel too deprived, something that can become a good eating pattern for life. You should retrain yourself to eat 3 sensible meals a day which are high in fiber, low in fat and sugar. Teach yourself not to nibble between meals. At the end of a successful diet, you should not be reaching for the chocolate cookies - in fact you should not think in terms of an end. During the diet you will hopefully not only have reshaped your figure, but also your eating habits.

The low calorie recipes in this book provide tempting yet imaginative ideas to help you provide a variety of tasty dishes that are good for your waistline too.

Using this book for a life long healthy eating plan

So in conclusion, the message is loud and clear. To maintain a healthy lifestyle eat less fat, particularly saturated fat, less sugar, less salt and more whole, fresh, fiber-rich cereals, fruit and vegetables. We should possibly learn to change the emphasis of our meals. The foods of animal

Healthy breakfasts can be tasty as well as low in calories.

origin should be eaten sparingly, and served as an accompaniment to a lavish selection of foods of vegetable origin.

The key to successfully fulfilling this plan is to eat a wide variety of foods. Packed full of deliciously healthy recipes, this book will ensure you'll never be stuck for choice.

There's no need to limit yourself to using just one or two sections of the book as they are all interchangeable. So have fun creating imaginative mix-and-match menus from the sugar-free, low salt, low cholesterol, vitamin rich and low calorie recipes, to ensure that you provide irresistibly tasty food which is reassuringly good for you.

LOW CHOLESTEROL

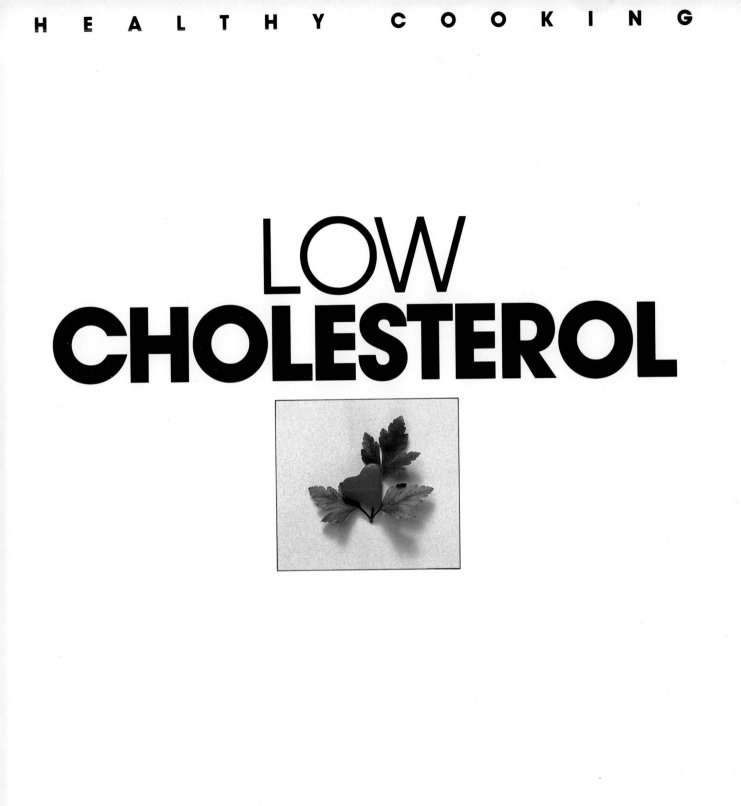

Introduction

Health and diet are inextricably linked to such a degree that none of us can afford to regard healthy eating simply as a fad. Heart disease in particular, is one of the most common fatal conditions in the Western world, and one of the most crucial factors which causes this is a high cholesterol diet.

Cholesterol is a fatty substance found in all animal tissue and it is also produced in the body by the liver. Essentially, cholesterol is needed to carry fats through the bloodstream. Problems occur when too much fat builds up and is left on the walls of arteries, narrowing them and restricting the blood flow around the body. If this flow becomes completely blocked, a heart attack will occur.

In order to reduce excess cholesterol we must change our eating habits by reducing the amount of animal tissue and animal fat which we eat.

Research has shown that by eating non-animal fats the blood levels of cholesterol can actually be reduced. The reason being that vegetable fats are mainly polyunsaturated and these help to regulate the blood flow and keep the arteries clear of fatty deposits. Polyunsaturated fats from vegetables can therefore be included freely in a low cholesterol diet but high fat animal products such as red meat, pork and dairy foods must be restricted. Fish contains a type of fat called mono-unsaturated, which has no effect on cholesterol levels and can therefore be included in your diet without any detrimental effect. Shellfish, however, are very high in cholesterol and should be avoided completely.

One point to watch out for is that some products, such as margarines, are not always as "healthy" as their packaging suggests. A production method called hydrogenation actually changes polyunsaturated fats into saturates, so look on labels and do not buy items which contain "hydrogenated vegetable oils" or "hydrogenated unsaturated fats."

These low cholesterol recipes have been developed to offer a wide choice of favorite items which combine healthy eating with flavor and variety. So delve inside and you will realize that as well as protecting your health, nutritious food can also tickle your taste buds.

SERVES 4-6

ONION SOUP

This delicious recipe demonstrates that food which is good for your heart need be neither bland nor boring.

¼ cup polyunsaturated margarine
2lbs onions, peeled and thinly sliced
3 tsps sugar
½ cup all-purpose flour
7½ cups chicken stock or water
Salt and freshly ground black pepper
1½ tsps dried thyme
½ cup dry white wine or dry sherry
12 x 1-inch slices French bread
3 tbsps olive oil
½ cup grated Cheddar cheese, optional
Fresh parsley for garnish

Step 1 Brown the onions in a large saucepan with the margarine and sugar.

1. Melt the margarine in a large saucepan. Stir in the onions and add the sugar. Cook uncovered over a low heat, stirring occasionally, for 15-20 minutes or until the onions become golden brown.

2. Stir the flour into the onions and cook for 1 minute.

3. Gradually pour the stock into the onions, mixing well with each addition to blend smoothly.

4. Season with the salt, pepper and thyme, and add the wine or sherry. Return the soup to a low heat and bring to the boil.

5. Partially cover the saucepan, then simmer the soup for 20-30 minutes.

6. Brush each side of the slices of bread lightly with the olive oil and arrange them on a metal rack in a broiler pan.

7. Lightly toast one side of the bread under a hot broiler until it turns pale gold.

Step 6 Lightly brush the slices of bread with the olive oil.

8. Turn the slices of bread over and sprinkle with the grated cheese, if used.

9. Return the slices of bread to the broiler and cook until the cheese has melted and is golden brown, or if the cheese is not being used, until the other side of the bread has been lightly toasted.

10. Serve the soup in individual bowls with 2 or 3 of the croutons floating on the top. Garnish with fresh parsley.

Cook's Notes

Time
Preparation takes about 20 minutes, cooking takes about 45 minutes-1 hour.

Freezing
This soup freezes very well, but the croutons should be prepared fresh each time.

Cook's Tip
The addition of sugar will help the onion to brown. For a paler soup, omit the sugar and gently fry the onions until they are just soft and not browned.

Fat Type
Chicken stock contains fairly small amounts of saturated fat. The cheese contains a higher amount, but is used in such small quantities that this should not matter. Use vegetable stock and omit the cheese if desired.

SERVES 4

CELERY AND APPLE SOUP

This interesting combination of flavors produces a tasty soup that is also suitable for vegetarians.

2 tbsps polyunsaturated margarine
1 large onion, peeled and finely chopped
3 cooking apples, peeled, cored and sliced
5 cups vegetable stock
1 bay leaf
Salt and freshly ground black pepper
3 sticks of celery, finely chopped
Finely sliced celery for garnish

Step 2 Gently cook the apples with the onion until it begins to soften.

1. Melt the margarine in a large pan and stir in the onions. Fry gently for 5 minutes, or until the onions are soft but not browned.

2. Add the apple to the onion mixture and cook for a further 3 minutes, or until the apple begins to soften.

3. Stir half the stock into the onion and apple, along with the bay leaf and seasoning. Bring the mixture to the boil, cover and simmer for half an hour. Remove the bay leaf.

4. Put the remaining stock into another pan along with the celery. Bring to the boil, then cover and simmer for 30 minutes.

5. Using a liquidizer or food processor, blend the onion and apple mixture until it is smooth.

6. Beat the puréed onion and apple mixture into the pan containing the stock and celery.

7. Return the pan to the heat and bring back to the boil. Garnish with the celery sticks and serve immediately

Step 4 Cook the celery in half of the stock, simmering until it is tender.

Step 6 Beat the puréed onion and apples into the stock and celery, mixing well to blend evenly.

Cook's Notes

Time
Preparation takes about 15 minutes, cooking takes about 45 minutes.

Serving Idea
Serve with whole-wheat rolls or a French stick.

Freezing
This recipe freezes well.

Fat Type
This recipe contains no saturated fat at all.

SERVES 6

MINESTRONE SOUP

There are numerous different recipes for minestrone. This one is high in fiber, which helps to reduce cholesterol levels in the blood, and it has hardly any saturated fats at all.

½ cup dried white cannellini beans
5 cups vegetable stock
3 tbsps olive oil
1 large onion, peeled and finely chopped
1 clove garlic, minced
1 stick celery, thinly sliced
2 carrots, peeled and diced
¼lb spring greens, finely shredded
½ cup cut green beans
1 large zucchini, trimmed and diced
¼lb tomatoes, peeled, seeded and diced
1 bay leaf
⅓ cup whole-wheat pasta
1½ tbsps fresh chopped basil
1½ tbsps fresh chopped parsley
Salt and freshly ground black pepper

1. Put the beans into a large bowl and cover with the vegetable stock. Leave to soak overnight. During this time the beans will double in volume.

2. Heat the oil in a large saucepan and gently fry the onion and garlic until they have softened, but not browned.

3. Stir in the celery, carrots, spring greens, green beans and zucchini. Fry gently, stirring until they have just began to soften.

4. Add the beans with the stock to the pan of vegetables, along with the tomatoes, bay leaf, pasta and seasoning. Bring to the boil, then cover and simmer for about 1 hour, or until the beans are very tender. Stir occasionally during this time to prevent the ingredients from sticking.

5. Stir in the basil and parsley, heat through for 5 minutes and serve immediately.

Step 1 Soak the beans overnight in the vegetable stock. They will double in volume during this time.

Step 4 Add the beans and stock to the partially cooked vegetables.

 Cook's Notes

 Time
Preparation takes about 20 minutes, plus overnight soaking for the beans. Cooking takes about 1½ hours.

 Serving Idea
Serve with crusty whole-wheat rolls.

Watchpoint
It is most important to cook any dried beans very thoroughly as they can be dangerous if eaten before they are sufficiently cooked.

 Variation
Use red kidney beans instead of the white cannellini beans in this recipe.

 Fat Type
Olive oil contains polyunsaturated fat and the pasta contains negligible amounts of saturated fat.

SERVES 4

VICHYSSOISE

Although this French soup is usually eaten cold, it also delicious served hot.

3 large leeks
2 tbsps polyunsaturated margarine
1 medium-sized onion, peeled and sliced
2 medium-sized potatoes, peeled and thinly sliced
2½ cups vegetable stock
Salt and ground white pepper
1¼ cups skim milk
Finely chopped parsley or chives, for garnish

1. Trim the top and bottom from the leeks and peel away the outer leaf.

2. Slit the leeks lengthwise down one side cutting right into the center of the vegetable.

3. Hold the leek under running cold water, allowing it to wash any bits of soil or grit from in between the leaves.

4. Slice the leeks very thinly using a sharp knife.

5. Melt the margarine in a saucepan and add the leek and sliced onion. Cover and allow to sweat gently over a low heat for about 10 minutes.

6. Add the potatoes to the leek mixture, and pour in the stock.

7. Season with the salt and pepper, cover and cook gently for 15 minutes, or until the potatoes are soft.

8. Using a liquidizer or food processor, purée the soup until it is smooth.

9. Return the puréed soup to the saucepan and stir in the milk. Adjust the seasoning and reheat very gently until it is almost boiling. Remove from heat.

10. Either serve the soup immediately or allow to cool, then chill in a refrigerator for at least 2 hours.

Step 2 Slit the leeks lengthwise down one side, cutting into the center of each vegetable.

Step 3 Hold the slit leeks under cold running water, allowing it to penetrate between the leaves to wash out any soil or grit.

Step 8 Purée the leek and potato mixture in a liquidizer or food processor, until it is very smooth.

11. Serve garnished with the finely chopped parsley or chives.

Cook's Notes

Time
Preparation takes about 15 minutes, plus chilling time. Cooking takes about 30 minutes.

Serving Idea
Serve with lightly toasted slices of whole-wheat bread.

Freezing
This soup freezes very well.

Fat Type
This soup contains a minimal amount of saturated fat in the milk.

SERVES 4

CHICKEN SATAY

This typical Indonesian dish is very spicy, but uses ingredients which are all low in fat, making it an excellent appetizer for four.

3 tbsps soy sauce
3 tbsps sesame oil
3 tbsps lime juice
1½ tsps ground cumin
1½ tsps turmeric powder
3 tsps ground coriander
1lb chicken breast, cut into 1-inch cubes
3 tbsps peanut oil
1 small onion, very finely chopped or minced
1½ tsps chili powder
½ cup crunchy peanut butter
1½ tsps brown sugar
Lime wedges and coriander leaves, for garnish

Step 5 Thread the marinated meat onto 4 large, or 8 small, kebab skewers.

Step 9 Brush the partially broiled chicken with a little of the peanut sauce to baste.

1. Put the soy sauce, sesame oil, lime juice, cumin, turmeric and coriander into a large bowl and mix well.

2. Add the cubed chicken to the soy sauce marinade and stir well to coat the meat evenly.

3. Cover with plastic wrap or a damp cloth and allow to stand in a refrigerator for at least 1 hour, but preferably overnight.

4. Drain the meat, reserving the marinade.

5. Thread the meat onto 4 large or 8 small skewers and set aside.

6. Heat the peanut oil in a small saucepan and add the onion and chili powder. Cook gently until the onion is slightly softened,

7. Stir the reserved marinade into the oil and onion mixture, along with the peanut butter and brown sugar. Heat gently, stirring constantly, until all the ingredients are well blended.

8. If the sauce is too thick, stir in 2-4 tbsps boiling water.

9. Arrange the skewers of meat on a broiler pan and cook under a preheated moderate broiler for 10-15 minutes. After the first 5 minutes of cooking, brush the skewered meat with a little of the peanut sauce to baste.

10. During the cooking time turn the meat frequently to cook it on all sides and prevent it browning.

11. Serve the skewered meat garnished with the lime and coriander leaves, and the remaining sauce separately.

Cook's Notes

 Time
Preparation takes about 25 minutes, cooking takes about 15 minutes.

 Serving Idea
Serve with a mixed salad.

 Variation
Use a selection of fresh vegetables instead of the chicken to make a vegetarian alternative, which would contain no saturated fat at all.

Fat Type
Chicken contains low amounts of saturated fat. The remaining ingredients contain unsaturated fats.

SERVES 4-6

SPICY VEGETABLE FRITTERS WITH TOMATO SAUCE

This delicious dish makes a ideal appetizer or interesting snack. Use any favorite vegetables or those that are in season.

1 cup all-purpose flour
1 cup whole-wheat flour
1½ tsps salt
1 tsp chili powder
1½ tsps ground cumin
1¼ cups water
1½ tbsps lemon juice
1 small cauliflower, broken into small flowerets
1 eggplant, cut into 1-inch cubes
3 zucchini, trimmed and cut into 1-inch pieces
2 cups button mushrooms
1 red pepper, seeded and cut into ¼-inch thick rounds
1 green pepper, seeded and cut into ¼-inch thick rounds
1 large potato, peeled and cut into 1-inch cubes
1⅔ cups canned plum tomatoes, drained
1 red chili, seeded and chopped
1 clove garlic, minced
1 small onion, peeled and finely chopped
1½ tbsps white wine vinegar
1½ tbsps soft brown sugar
Salt the freshly ground black pepper, to taste
1 sliced green chili for garnish
1 sliced red chili for garnish

1. Put the flours, salt, chili powder and cumin into a large bowl. Make a slight well in the center.

2. Gradually add the water and lemon juice to the flour, beating well until a smooth batter is formed.

3. Wash the fresh vegetables and allow them to drain completely on paper towels or a clean cloth.

4. Put the tomatoes, fresh chili, garlic, onions, vinegar and sugar into a food processor or liquidizer and blend until the sauce is smooth.

5. Pour the sauce mixture into a small pan and heat gently, stirring until it is completely warmed through. Season with salt and transfer to a small serving dish and garnish with slices of red and green chilies.

6. Heat some vegetable oil in a deep fat fryer until it is warm enough to brown a 1-inch cube of bread in just under 1 minute.

7. Make sure the vegetables are completely dry, patting any moisture off them with paper towels if necessary.

8. Using a slotted spoon drop the vegetables, a few at a time, into the batter and dip them to coat thoroughly.

9. Remove the vegetables from the batter, again using the slotted spoon, and allow some of the batter to drain back into the bowl.

10. Drop the vegetables into the hot oil, and fry quickly until they are golden brown and the batter puffy.

11. Remove the fried vegetables from the oil and drain completely on paper towels, keeping them warm until all the remaining vegetables have been prepared in this manner.

12. Serve immediately, providing small forks with which to dip the vegetables into the spicy tomato sauce.

Cook's Notes

 Time
Preparation takes about 20 minutes, cooking takes about ½ hour.

! **Watchpoint**
It is important to ensure that the vegetables are completely dry before coating with the batter, or it will not cover them.

 Fat Type
There is no saturated fat in this dish, but it is important to check that the oil used in the deep fat frying is polyunsaturated and that it is fresh.

SERVES 6

TUNA, BEAN AND TOMATO SALAD

Fish is of great value in a low cholesterol diet as it contains mono-unsaturated fats which do not affect the cholesterol level in the blood.

1 cup dried flageolet beans
6oz canned tuna in brine
Juice of 1 lemon
⅔ cup olive oil
1½ tsps chopped fresh herbs, e.g. parsley, basil or marjoram
Salt and freshly ground black pepper
8 firm tomatoes

1. Put the beans into a bowl and pour over enough cold water to just cover. Allow to soak overnight.

2. Drain the beans and put them into a saucepan. Cover with boiling water, then simmer for at least 1 hour. Drain thoroughly and cool.

3. Drain the can of tuna and flake it into a bowl.

4. Put the lemon juice, olive oil, herbs and seasoning into a small bowl and beat together with a fork.

5. Stir the beans into the tuna fish and mix in the dressing, tossing the salad together carefully so that the tuna does not break up too much, but the dressing is thoroughly incorporated.

6. Adjust the seasoning and arrange the salad in a mound on a shallow serving dish.

7. Cut a small cross into the skins of the tomato and plunge them into boiling water for 30 seconds.

8. Using a sharp knife carefully peel away the skins from the tomatoes.

9. Slice the tomatoes thinly and arrange them around the edge of the bean and tuna salad. Serve immediately.

Step 5 Mix the dressing into the salad by tossing it carefully, to ensure that the tuna does not break up too much.

Step 8 When blanched, the skins on the tomatoes should peel away very easily if you use a sharp knife.

Cook's Notes

 Time
Preparation takes about 25 minutes, plus overnight soaking.

 **Watchpoint**
Great care must be taken with cooking beans, as any that are under cooked could be dangerous when eaten.

 Fat Type
This recipe contains mono-unsaturated and polyunsaturated fats.

 Variation
Use any type of bean of your choice.

 Serving Idea
Serve with a simple lettuce salad.

SERVES 4

SMOKED MACKEREL PÂTÉ

Smoked fish has a wonderful flavor and is ideal for making pâté.

8oz smoked mackerel fillets, skin and bones removed
¼ cup polyunsaturated margarine
Juice of half an orange
1½ tsps tomato paste
1½ tsps white wine vinegar
Salt and freshly ground black pepper, optional
1 x 3½ oz can pimento peppers, drained
1¼ cups clear vegetable stock
3 tsps powdered gelatin
3 tbsps dry sherry
3 tbsps cold water

Step 3 Arrange the strips of pimento in a lattice pattern over the top of the pâté.

1. Put the mackerel, margarine, orange juice, paste, vinegar and seasonings into a liquidizer or food processor and blend until smooth.

2. Put the pâté into a serving dish and smooth the top evenly.

3. Cut the pimentos into thin strips and arrange in a lattice over the top of the pâté.

4. Bring the stock to the boil in a small pan. Remove from the heat and cool for 1 minute.

5. Sprinkle over the gelatin and allow to stand, stirring occasionally until it has completely dissolved.

6. When the gelatin has dissolved the liquid should be

Step 5 Sprinkle the gelatine over the hot stock and allow it to stand, to dissolve completely.

clear. At this point stir in the sherry and cold water.

7. Very carefully spoon the aspic over the top of the mackerel pâté and the pimentos, taking great care not to dislodge the lattice pattern.

8. Chill the pâté in a refrigerator until the aspic has completely set.

COOK'S NOTES

Time
Preparation takes about 30 minutes, plus chilling time. Cooking takes about 2 minutes.

Variation
Use any type of smoked fish in place of the mackerel in this recipe.

Preparation
If you do not have a food processor or blender, this pâté can be made by mashing with a fork, but it will not have such a smooth texture.

Fat Type
Fish contains mono-unsaturated fat which does not affect the cholesterol level in the blood.

Serving Idea
Serve with crusty whole-wheat bread or French toast.

SERVES 4-6

TOMATO AND PEPPER ICE

Similar to frozen gazpacho, this appetizer is ideal for serving on warm summer days. It could also be used, in smaller quantities, as a palate freshener between courses in place of a conventional sweet sorbet.

6 ice cubes
½ cup canned tomato juice
Juice 1 lemon
1½ tsps Worcestershire sauce
½ small green pepper, seeded and roughly chopped
½ small red pepper, seeded and roughly chopped

1. Break the ice into small pieces using a small hammer.

2. Put the broken ice into a blender or food processor, along with the tomato juice, lemon juice and Worcestershire sauce. Blend the mixture until it becomes slushy.

3. Pour the tomato mixture into ice trays and freeze for ½ hour, or until it is just half frozen.

4. Using a sharp knife, chop the peppers into very small pieces.

5. Remove the tomato ice from the freezer trays and put it into a bowl.

6. Mash the tomato ice with the back of a fork until the crystals are well broken up.

7. Mix in the chopped peppers and return the tomato ice to the freezer trays.

8. Re-freeze for a further 1½ hours, stirring occasionally to prevent the mixture from solidifying completely.

9. To serve, allow the tomato ice to defrost for about 5 minutes, then mash with the back of a fork to roughly break up the ice crystals. Serve in small glass dishes which have been chilled beforehand.

Step 2 Blend the ice, tomato juice, lemon juice and Worcestershire sauce until it becomes a smooth slush.

Step 6 Mash the semi-frozen tomato ice with the back of a fork to break up the ice crystals finely.

Step 8 During the freezing time, keep stirring the tomato and pepper ice with a fork, to prevent the mixture from becoming a solid block.

Cook's Notes

Time
Preparation takes about 15 minutes, plus freezing time.

Freezing
This recipe will freeze for up to 2 months.

Watchpoint
Take care not to allow the tomato ice to freeze into a solid block, or it will be too hard to break into rough crystals.

Serving Idea
Scoop out the tomatoes and serve this ice in the shells, instead of glass dishes.

Fat Type
There is no fat in this recipe.

SERVES 4

SUMMER PASTA SALAD

Lightly cooked summer vegetables and whole-wheat pasta are combined to create this delicious wholesome salad.

1 eggplant
1 zucchini
1 red pepper
1 green pepper
1 medium-sized onion
2 large tomatoes
6 tbsps olive oil
1 clove garlic, minced
Salt and freshly ground black pepper
1⅓ cups whole-wheat pasta spirals
1½ tbsps vinegar
¾ tsp dry English mustard

Step 1 Sprinkle the eggplant slices liberally with salt and allow them to degorge for 30 minutes to remove their bitterness.

1. Cut the eggplant into ½-inch slices. Sprinkle the slices liberally with salt and allow to stand for 30 minutes.

2. Using a sharp knife, trim the zucchini and cut into ¼-inch slices.

3. Cut the peppers in half and carefully remove the cores and seeds. Using a sharp knife, cut the pepper into thin strips.

4. Peel and finely chop the onion.

5. Cut a small cross in the skins of the tomatoes and plunge them into boiling water for 30 seconds. After this time remove the tomatoes and carefully peel away the skins.

6. Cut the peeled tomatoes into 8. Remove and discard the pips from each tomato slice.

7. Put 3 tbsps of the olive oil in a frying pan and stir in the onion. Fry gently until it is transparent, but not colored.

8. Thoroughly rinse the salt from the eggplant slices and pat them dry on absorbent paper towels. Roughly chop the slices.

9. Add the chopped eggplant, zucchini, peppers, tomatoes and garlic to the cooked onion and fry very

Step 9 Gently fry all the vegetables together, stirring frequently to prevent them from browning.

gently for 20 minutes, or until just soft. Season with salt and pepper and allow to cool.

10. Put the pasta spirals in a large saucepan and cover with boiling water. Sprinkle in a little salt and simmer for 10 minutes or until tender but still firm.

11. Rinse the pasta in cold water and drain very well.

12. Beat together the remaining olive oil, the vinegar and mustard in a small bowl. Season with salt and pepper.

13. Put the pasta and cooled vegetables into a serving dish and pour over the dressing, tossing the ingredients together to coat them evenly. Serve well chilled.

 — Cook's Notes —

 Time
Preparation takes approximately 40 minutes, cooking takes 30 minutes.

 Preparation
Make sure that the eggplant is rinsed very thoroughly or the salad will be much too salty.

Fat Type
Olive oil contains polyunsaturated fat and is therefore beneficial to those on a low cholesterol diet.

SERVES 4

MUSHROOM PASTA SALAD

Mushrooms are always delicious in a salad and this recipe, which combines them with whole-wheat pasta shapes, is no exception.

7½ tbsps olive oil
Juice of 2 lemons
1½ tsps fresh chopped basil
1½ tsps fresh chopped parsley
Salt and freshly ground black pepper
2 cups mushrooms
1⅓ cups whole-wheat pasta shapes of your choice

boiling water. Season with a little salt and simmer for 10 minutes, or until just tender.

5. Rinse the pasta in cold water and drain well.

6. Add the pasta to the marinated mushrooms and lemon dressing, mixing well to coat evenly.

7. Adjust the seasoning if necessary, then chill well before serving.

Step 1 Beat the lemon juice, herbs and seasoning together in a large bowl using a fork.

Step 2 Use a sharp knife to slice the mushrooms thinly.

1. In a large bowl mix together the olive oil, lemon juice, herbs and seasoning.

2. Finely slice the mushrooms and add these to the lemon dressing in the bowl, stirring well to coat the mushrooms evenly.

3. Cover the bowl with plastic wrap and allow to stand in a cool place for at least 1 hour.

4. Put the pasta into a large saucepan and cover with

Step 6 Stir the cooled pasta into the marinated mushrooms, mixing well to coat evenly.

Cook's Notes

Time
Preparation takes approximately 10 minutes, plus 1 hour at least for the mushrooms to marinate. Cooking takes about 15 minutes.

Variation
Use a mixture of button and wild mushrooms for a delicious variation in flavor.

Serving Idea
Serve mushroom pasta salad on a bed of mixed lettuce.

Fat Type
Olive oil contains polyunsaturated fat and is beneficial for those on a low cholesterol diet.

SERVES 4-6

STIR-FRY TOFU SALAD

Ideal for vegetarians, but so delicious that it will be enjoyed by everyone.

1 cake of tofu
¼lb snow peas
½ cup mushrooms
2 carrots, peeled
2 sticks celery
½ cup broccoli flowerets
⅔ cup vegetable oil
4½ tbsps lemon juice
3 tsps honey
1½ tsps grated fresh ginger
4½ tbsps soy sauce
Dash of sesame oil
4 green onions
½ cup unsalted roasted peanuts
1 cup bean sprouts
½ head Chinese cabbage

1. Drain the tofu well and press gently to remove any excess moisture. Cut into ½-inch cubes.

2. Trim the tops and tails from the snow peas.

3. Thinly slice the mushrooms with a sharp knife.

4. Cut the carrots and celery into thin slices, angling your knife so that each slice is cut on the diagonal.

5. Trim the green onions and slice them in the same way as the carrots and celery.

6. Heat 3 tbsps of the vegetable oil in a wok or large frying pan. Stir in the snow peas, mushrooms, celery, carrots and broccoli, and cook for 2 minutes, stirring constantly.

7. Remove the vegetables from the wok and set them aside to cool.

8. Put the remaining oil into a small bowl and beat in the lemon juice, honey, ginger, soy sauce and sesame oil.

9. Stir the sliced green onions, peanuts and bean sprouts into the cooled vegetables.

10. Mix the dressing into the salad vegetables, then add the tofu. Toss the tofu into the salad very carefully so that it does not break up.

11. Shred the Chinese cabbage and arrange them on a serving platter. Pile the salad ingredients over the top and serve well chilled.

Step 4 Slice the carrots and celery thinly, cutting with your knife at an angle to produce diagonal pieces

Step 10 Toss the tofu very carefully into the salad ingredients taking care not the break it up.

Cook's Notes

Time
Preparation takes approximately 25 minutes, cooking takes 2-4 minutes.

Preparation
Make sure that the stir-fried vegetables are completely cool before adding the remaining salad ingredients, or they will lose their crispness.

Variation
Shredded cooked chicken can be used in place of the tofu in this recipe.

Fat Type
All the fat in this recipe is polyunsaturated.

SERVES 6-8

MIXED PEPPER SALAD

It is now possible to buy sweet peppers in a variety of colors, so include as many as you wish in this eye-catching salad.

3 red peppers
3 green peppers
3 yellow peppers
3 tbsps vegetable oil
9 tbsps sunflower oil
3 tbsps lemon juice
3 tbsps white wine vinegar
1 small clove garlic, minced
Pinch salt
Pinch cayenne pepper
Pinch sugar
3 hard-cooked eggs
⅓ cup black olives, pitted
3 tbsps finely chopped fresh coriander leaves, optional

1. Cut all the peppers in half and remove the seeds and cores.

2. With the palm of your hand lightly press the halved peppers down onto a flat surface, to flatten them out.

3. Brush the skin side of each pepper with a little of the vegetable oil and place under a preheated hot broiler.

4. Cook until the skins begin to char and split.

5. Remove the peppers from the broiler and wrap them in a clean dishtowel. Allow to stand for 10-15 minutes.

6. Put the sunflower oil, lemon juice, vinegar, garlic, salt, pepper and sugar into a small bowl and beat together well.

7. Shell the eggs and cut each one into four.

Step 2 Put the cored pepper halves cut side down on a flat surface and gently press them with the palm of your hand to flatten them out.

Step 4 Cook the oiled peppers under the broiler until the skin begins to char and split.

8. Unwrap the peppers and carefully peel away the burnt skin. Cut the pepper flesh into thick strips about 1-inch wide.

9. Arrange the pepper strips in a circle, alternating the colors all the way round.

10. Arrange the olives and quartered eggs in the center.

11. Sprinkle with the coriander leaves, and spoon over all the dressing.

12. Chill the salad for at least 1 hour before serving.

Cook's Notes

Time
Preparation takes 20 minutes, cooking takes about 5 minutes.

Serving Idea
Serve this salad with crusty French bread or rolls.

Cook's Tip
Peeled peppers will keep in a refrigerator for up to 5 days if they are covered with a little oil.

Fat Type
This recipe is high in polyunsaturated fats. The eggs contain saturated fats, but can be omitted if desired.

SERVES 4

CHEESY STUFFED TOMATOES

Although cheese should be avoided on a low fat diet, soft cheeses such as Brie and Camembert do have a lower fat content than Cheddar and in small amounts can provide welcome variety in a restricted diet.

4 beefsteak tomatoes
4 anchovy fillets
3 tsps capers, drained
2 green onions
1 cup Camembert or Brie cheese, rind removed
3 tsps caraway seeds
Salt and freshly ground black pepper
Lettuce to garnish

1. Cut a slice from the rounded end of each tomato and carefully scoop out the pulp and seeds. Strain out the seeds and reserve the pulp and juice for the filling.

Step 1 Strain the seeds out of the tomato pulp, keeping only the pulp and juice for use in the recipe.

2. Put the anchovies in a bowl and cover with a little milk. Allow to soak for 5 minutes to remove the saltiness.

3. Drain and rinse the anchovies, then pat them dry. Chop the anchovies finely.

4. Put the capers and green onions onto a board and chop them finely also.

5. Put the cheese into a bowl and mash it with a fork.

6. Stir in the capers, anchovies, onions, caraway seeds, tomato juice and pulp. Mix together thoroughly, then season with a little salt and pepper.

7. Carefully spoon the cheese filling into the hollowed out tomatoes and arrange them on a serving plate.

Step 7 Carefully pile the cheese filling back into the hollowed out tomatoes.

8. Replace the sliced tops and serve them well chilled on a bed of lettuce.

 Cook's Notes

 Time
Preparation takes 15 minutes, plus chilling time of at least 1 hour.

 Preparation
Use a grapefruit knife or serrated teaspoon to remove the centers of the tomatoes.

Variation
Use cottage or curd cheese instead of the Camembert or Brie.

 Serving Idea
Serve with a vinaigrette dressing and whole-wheat bread or rolls.

 Fat Type
The cheese contains saturated fat, so should only be eaten in moderation.

SERVES 4

MEDITERRANEAN EGGPLANTS

These delicious stuffed eggplants can be served as an accompaniment to a main meal for four or as a lunch dish for two.

2 small eggplants
2 tbsps polyunsaturated margarine
1 small onion, finely chopped
1 clove garlic, minced
¼lb tomatoes
⅔ cup long grain rice, cooked
3 tsps fresh chopped marjoram
Pinch cinnamon
Salt and freshly ground black pepper

1. Preheat an oven to 350°F. Wrap the eggplants in aluminum foil and bake for 20 minutes to soften. Allow to cool.

2. Cut the eggplants in half, then using a serrated teaspoon or grapefruit knife, carefully scoop out the pulp leaving a ½-inch border to form a shell.

3. Melt the margarine in a frying pan and gently sauté the

onion and garlic until they are just soft.

4. Chop the eggplant pulp roughly and stir into the pan along with the onions. Cover and cook for about 5 minutes.

5. Cut a small cross in the skins of the tomatoes and plunge them into boiling water for 30 seconds.

6. Remove the tomatoes from the water and carefully peel away the skin using a sharp knife.

7. Quarter the tomatoes and remove and discard the pips. Chop the tomato flesh roughly and stir into the cooked eggplant and onion mixture, along with the rice, marjoram and cinnamon. Season with salt and pepper.

8. Carefully pile the rice filling back into the eggplant shells and arrange them on an ovenproof dish or cookie sheet. Cover with aluminum foil.

9. Return to the oven and bake for 20 minutes. Serve hot, garnished with a little finely chopped parsley if desired.

Step 2 Carefully scoop the pulp out of each eggplant half with a serrated spoon or grapefruit knife, leaving a thin border on the inside to form a shell.

Step 7 Remove and discard the seeds from the peeled tomatoes.

Cook's Notes

Time
Preparation takes 25 minutes, cooking takes about 40 minutes.

Preparation
Take care not to split the eggplant shells when scooping out the pulp.

Variation
½ cup mature Cheddar cheese can be added to the filling if desired or allowed!

Fat Type
This recipe contains only polyunsaturated fats.

SERVES 4

CHICKEN WITH "BURNT" PEPPERS AND CORIANDER

"Burning" peppers is a technique for removing the skins which also imparts a delicious flavor to this favorite vegetable.

2 red peppers, halved and seeded
1 green pepper, halved and seeded
6 tbsps vegetable oil, for brushing
1½ tbsps olive oil
3 tsps paprika
Pinch ground cumin
Pinch cayenne pepper
2 cloves garlic, minced
1lb canned tomatoes, drained and chopped
4½ tbsps fresh chopped coriander
4½ tbsps fresh chopped parsley
Salt, for seasoning
4 large chicken breasts, boned
1 large onion, sliced
⅓ cup slivered almonds

1. Put the peppers, cut side down, on a flat surface and gently press them with the palm of your hand to flatten them out.

2. Brush the skin side with 3 tbsps of the vegetable oil and cook them under a hot broiler until the skin chars and splits.

3. Wrap the peppers in a clean towel for 10 minutes to cool.

4. Unwrap the peppers and carefully peel off the charred skin. Chop the pepper flesh into thin strips.

5. Heat the olive oil in a frying pan and gently fry the paprika, cumin, cayenne pepper and garlic for 2 minutes, stirring to prevent the garlic from browning.

6. Stir in the tomatoes, coriander, parsley and season with a little salt. Simmer for 15-20 minutes, or until thick. Set aside.

7. Heat the remaining vegetable oil in an ovenproof casserole dish, and sauté the chicken breasts, turning them frequently until they are golden brown on both sides.

8. Remove the chicken and set aside. Gently fry the onions in the oil for about 5 minutes, or until softened but not overcooked.

9. Return the chicken to the casserole with the onions and pour on about 1¼ cups of water. Bring to the boil.

10. Cover the casserole and simmer for about 30 minutes, turning the chicken occasionally to prevent it from burning.

11. Remove the chicken from the casserole and boil the remaining liquid rapidly to reduce to about ⅓ cup of stock.

12. Add the peppers and the tomato sauce to the chicken stock and stir well.

13. Return the chicken to the casserole, cover and simmer very gently for a further 30 minutes, or until the chicken is tender.

14. Arrange the chicken on a serving dish with a little of the sauce spooned over. Sprinkle with the almonds and serve any remaining sauce separately.

Cook's Notes

Time
Preparation takes 30 minutes, cooking takes about 1 hour 30 minutes.

Preparation
Take care not to cook this dish too rapidly or the peppers will disintegrate.

Fat Type
The chicken contains saturated fats, but only in small quantities, the rest of the dish contains only polyunsaturated fat.

SERVES 4

HERRINGS WITH APPLES

The addition of fresh tasting apples beautifully complements the delicious and wholesome flavor of herring.

4 herrings, cleaned
2 large dessert apples
1 large onion
4 large potatoes, peeled and sliced
Salt and freshly ground black pepper
½ cup dry cider
1 cup dried breadcrumbs
¼ cup polyunsaturated margarine
1½ tbsps fresh chopped parsley

1. Cut the heads and tails from the herrings and split them open from the underside.

2. Put the herrings, belly side down, on a flat surface and carefully press along the back of each fish with the palm of your hand, pushing the backbone down towards the surface.

3. Turn the herrings over and with a sharp knife, carefully prise away the backbone, pulling out any loose bones as you go. Do not cut the fish into separate fillets. Wash and dry them well.

4. Peel, quarter, core and slice one of the apples. Peel and slice the onion thinly.

5. Lightly grease a shallow baking pan and layer with the potatoes, apple and onions, seasoning well with salt and pepper between layers.

6. Pour the cider over the potato layers and cover the dish with foil. Bake in a preheated oven 350°F for 40 minutes.

7. Remove the dish from the oven and arrange the herring fillets over the top.

8. Sprinkle the breadcrumbs over the herrings and dot

Step 2 Press down the backbone of the herrings with the palm of your hand, pushing the spine towards the work surface as you go.

Step 3 Carefully lift the backbone away from the fish with a sharp knife, pulling any loose bones out at the same time. Do not cut the fish into separate fillets.

with half of the margarine.

9. Increase the oven temperature to 400°F and return the dish to the oven for about 10–15 minutes, or until the herrings are cooked and brown.

10. Core the remaining apples and slice into rounds, leaving the peel on.

11. Melt the remaining margarine in a frying pan and gently fry the apple slices.

12. Remove the herrings from the oven and garnish with the fried apple slices and chopped parsley. Serve at once.

Cook's Notes

Time
Preparation takes 15-20 minutes, cooking takes about 50 minutes.

Variation
Use small mackerel instead of herrings in this recipe.

Serving Idea
Serve with a carrot, orange and watercress salad.

Fat Type
Fish contains mono-unsaturated fats which do not affect the cholesterol levels in the blood.

SERVES 6-8

SALMON TROUT WITH SPINACH AND WALNUT STUFFING

1 fresh whole salmon trout, weighing 2½lbs, cleaned
2lbs fresh spinach
1 small onion
¼ cup polyunsaturated margarine
½ cup walnuts, roughly chopped
2 cups fresh white breadcrumbs
1½ tbsps fresh chopped parsley
1½ tbsps fresh chopped thyme
Pinch grated nutmeg
Salt and freshly ground black pepper
Juice 2 lemons
Watercress sprigs and lemon slices, to garnish

1. Carefully cut the underside of the fish from the end of the slit made when the fish was cleaned, to the tip of the tail.

2. Place the fish, belly side down, on a flat work surface, spreading the cut underside out to balance the fish more easily.

3. Using the palm of your hand press down along the backbone of the fish, pushing the spine downwards towards the work surface.

4. Turn the fish over and using a sharp knife, carefully pull the backbone away from the fish, cutting it away with scissors at the base of the head and tail.

5. Remove the backbone completely and pull out any loose bones you may find with a pair of tweezers. Lay the boned fish in the center of a large square of lightly oiled aluminum foil and set aside.

6. Wash the spinach leaves well and tear off any coarse stalks. Put the spinach into a large saucepan and sprinkle

with salt. Do not add any extra water. Cover and cook over a moderate heat for about 3 minutes.

7. Turn the spinach into a colander and drain well, pressing with the back of a wooden spoon to remove all the excess moisture.

8. Chop the cooked spinach very finely using a sharp knife.

9. Peel and chop the onion finely and fry gently in about 1 tbsp of the margarine until soft, but not colored.

10. Stir the cooked onion into the chopped spinach along with the walnuts, breadcrumbs, herbs, nutmeg, salt, pepper and half of the lemon juice. Mix well to blend evenly.

11. Use the spinach stuffing to fill the cavity inside the trout. Push the stuffing in firmly, re-shaping the fish as you do so. Allow a little of the stuffing to show between the cut edge of the fish.

12. Seal the foil over the top of the fish, but do not wrap it too tightly.

13. Place the fish in a roasting pan and bake in a preheated oven at 350°F for 35 minutes.

14. Carefully unwrap the fish and transfer it to a large serving dish.

15. Using a sharp knife, peel away the skin from all exposed sides of the fish. If possible remove some skin from the underside also.

16. Whilst the fish is still hot, dot with the remaining margarine, sprinkle with the remaining lemon juice, then serve garnished with the watercress and sliced lemon.

Cook's Notes

Time
Preparation takes 35-40 minutes, cooking takes about 40 minutes.

Cook's Tip
If you feel that you cannot bone the fish yourself, ask your fishmonger to do it for you, but explain that you wish the bone to be removed from the underside of the fish.

Fat Type
Fish contains mono-unsaturated fats and the remainder of fats used in this recipe are all polyunsaturated.

SERVES 4

SPANISH GUINEA FOWL

The olive oil in this recipe gives a wonderful flavor to the sauce without loading it with saturated fat.

4 small guinea fowl
Salt and freshly ground black pepper
Olive oil, to brush
4 small wedges of lime or lemon
4 bay leaves
3 tbsps olive oil
1 small onion, thinly sliced
1 clove garlic, peeled and minced
1lb tomatoes
⅔ cup red wine
⅔ cup chicken or vegetable stock
1½ tbsps tomato paste
1 green chilies, seeded and thinly sliced
1 small red pepper, seeded and cut into thin strips
1 small green pepper, seeded and cut into thin strips
3 tbsps chopped blanched almonds
1½ tbsps pine kernels
12 small black olives, pitted
1½ tbsps raisins

1. Rub the guinea fowl inside and out with salt and pepper. Brush the skins with olive oil and push a wedge of lemon or lime, and a bay leaf into the center of each one.

2. Roast the guinea fowl, uncovered, in a preheated oven 375°F for 45 minutes, or until just tender.

3. Heat the 3 tbsps olive oil in a large frying pan and gently cook the onion and the garlic until they are soft, but not colored.

4. Cut a slit into the skins of each tomato and plunge into boiling water for 30 seconds.

5. Using a sharp knife carefully peel away the skins from the blanched tomatoes.

6. Chop the tomatoes roughly. Remove and discard the seeds and cores.

7. Add the chopped tomatoes to the cooked onion and garlic, and fry gently for a further 2 minutes.

8. Add all the remaining ingredients and simmer for 10-15 minutes, or until the tomatoes have completely softened and the sauce has thickened slightly.

9. Arrange the guinea fowl on a serving dish and spoon a little of the sauce over each one.

10. Serve hot with the remaining sauce in a separate jug.

Step 3 Fry the onion and garlic gently in the olive oil until they are soft but not colored.

Step 5 Using a sharp knife carefully peel away the loosened skins from the blanched tomatoes.

Cook's Notes

Time
Preparation takes 15 minutes, cooking takes about 1 hour.

Serving Idea
Serve with rice and a mixed green salad.

Cook's Tip
If the guinea fowl start to get too brown during the cooking time, cover them with aluminum foil.

Fat Type
Chicken contains only small amounts of saturated fats, and the remaining ingredients in this recipe contain only unsaturated fats.

SERVES 4

SAFFRON CHICKEN

The delicate color and flavor of saffron enhances the taste of chicken and gives this dish a Mediterranean flavor.

2-3lb chicken
3 tbsps olive oil
Salt and freshly ground black pepper
1 small onion, peeled and finely chopped
1 clove garlic, minced
3 tsps paprika
8 tomatoes
1½ cups long grain white rice
2½ cups boiling water
Large pinch saffron strands or ¼ tsp ground saffron
1 cup frozen peas
3 tbsps chopped fresh parsley

Step 4 Remove the skin from the chicken joints by pulling and cutting with a sharp knife.

1. Cut the chicken into 8 pieces with a sharp knife or cook's cleaver, cutting lengthwise down the breast bone and through the backbone, to halve it completely.

2. Cut the chicken halves in half again, slitting between the leg joint diagonally up and around the breast joint.

3. Finally cut each chicken quarter in half by cutting away the drumsticks from the leg thigh joint, and the wings from the breast joints.

4. Remove the skin from the chicken joints by pulling and cutting with a sharp knife.

5. Heat the oil in a large casserole dish or sauté pan, and fry the chicken, turning it frequently to brown evenly. Season with a little salt and pepper, then remove it from the pan and set aside.

6. Add the onions and garlic to the juices in the sauté pan and cook slowly until softened but not colored.

7. Add the paprika to the onions and fry quickly for about

30 seconds to just burn.

8. Cut a small cross into the skins of the tomatoes and plunge them into boiling water.

9. Using a sharp knife peel away the loosened skin from each tomato.

10. Cut the tomatoes into quarters and remove the cores and seeds. Chop the tomato flesh finely and add this to the sauté pan with the paprika and the onions.

11. Cook for about 5-10 minutes to draw off the liquid from the tomatoes. The sauce mixture should be of a dropping consistency when this has been done.

12. Stir the rice, water and saffron into the tomato purée along with the browned chicken portions. Bring to the boil, reduce the heat to simmering, then cover the casserole tightly and cook for about 20 minutes.

13. Add the peas and the parsley to the casserole, stir well and continue cooking for a further 5-10 minutes, or until the rice is tender and all the liquids have been absorbed.

14. Serve very hot.

 Cook's Notes

Time
Preparation takes about 25 minutes, cooking takes 30-35 minutes.

Watchpoint
Stir the casserole frequently after step 12 to prevent the rice from sticking.

Fat Type
Chicken contains small amounts of saturated fat, but the remainder in this recipe is polyunsaturated.

SERVES 4

CHICKEN LIVER STIR-FRY

Chicken livers are very low in fat and high in flavor. They also require very little cooking so are perfect for stir-fry recipes.

1lb chicken livers
4½ tbsps sesame oil
⅓ cup split blanched almonds
1 clove garlic, peeled
⅓ cup snow peas, trimmed
8-10 Chinese cabbage leaves, shredded
3 tsps cornstarch
1½ tbsps cold water
3 tbsps soy sauce
⅔ cup chicken or vegetable stock

1. Trim the chicken livers, removing any discolored areas or fatty tubes.

2. Cut the chicken livers into even-sized pieces.

3. Heat a wok and pour in the oil. When the oil is hot, reduce the heat and stir-fry the almonds until they are pale golden brown. Remove the almonds, draining any oil back into the wok, and set them aside on kitchen towels.

4. Add the garlic clove to the wok and cook for 1-2 minutes to flavor the oil only. Remove the clove of garlic and discard.

5. Stir the chicken livers into the flavored oil and cook for 2-3 minutes, stirring frequently to brown evenly. Remove the chicken livers from the wok and set them aside.

6. Add the snow peas to the hot oil and stir-fry for 1 minute. Then stir in the Chinese cabbage leaves and cook for 1 minute further. Remove the vegetables and set aside.

7. Mix together the cornstarch and water, then blend in the soy sauce and stock.

8. Pour the cornstarch mixture into the wok and bring to the boil, stirring until the sauce has thickened and cleared.

Step 1 Trim the chicken livers, cutting away any discolored areas or bits of fat or tubes using a sharp knife.

Step 3 Stir-fry the almonds in the hot oil until they are a pale golden brown.

Step 8 Cook the sauce in the wok, stirring all the time until it has thickened and cleared.

9. Return all other ingredients to the wok and heat through for 1 minute. Serve immediately.

Cook's Notes

Time
Preparation takes 25 minutes, cooking takes 5-6 minutes.

Variation
Use finely sliced lamb or calves' liver in place of the chicken livers.

Serving Idea
Serve with fried rice or noodles.

Fat Type
Liver contains saturated fat, but in very small quantities.

SERVES 4-6

CHICKEN WITH LEMON JULIENNE

Lean chicken served with a tangy julienne of fresh vegetables makes a delicious main course – ideal for those on a low cholesterol diet.

1 x 3lb chicken
3 tbsps olive oil
3 tbsps polyunsaturated margarine
2 sticks celery
2 carrots
1 small onion, peeled and thinly sliced
1½ tbsps chopped fresh basil
1 bay leaf
Juice and grated rind of 2 small lemons
⅔ cup water
Salt and freshly ground black pepper
Pinch sugar, optional
Lemon slices for garnish

1. Cut the chicken into 8 pieces with a sharp knife or a cook's cleaver, cutting the chicken lengthwise down the breastbone and through the backbone to halve it completely.

2. Cut the chicken halves in half again, slitting between the leg joint diagonally up and around the breast joint.

3. Finally cut each chicken quarter in half by cutting away the drumsticks from the leg thigh joint, and the wings from the breast joints.

4. Remove the skin from the chicken joints by pulling and cutting with a sharp knife.

5. Heat the oil in a large sauté pan along with the margarine. Gently fry the chicken pieces, turning them frequently to brown evenly.

6. Remove the chicken pieces to a plate and set aside.

7. Using a sharp knife cut the celery into pieces 1½-inches long. Cut these pieces into long thin matchsticks lengthwise.

8. Cut the carrots into similar length pieces, then cut each piece in half lengthwise. Continue cutting each carrot half into the same sized pieces as the celery.

9. Stir the carrots and celery into the chicken juices, along with the onion. Cook over a gentle heat for about 3 minutes or until just beginning to soften but not brown.

10. Stir the basil, bay leaf, lemon juice and rind, the water, salt and pepper into the vegetables, mix well and cook for 2-3 minutes.

11. Return the chicken portions to the casserole and bring the mixture to the boil.

12. Cover the pan and reduce the heat. Allow the casserole to simmer for about 35-45 minutes, or until the chicken is tender and the juices will run clear when the meat is pierced with a sharp knife.

13. Remove the chicken and vegetables to a serving dish and discard the bay leaf.

14. Heat the sauce quickly to thicken if necessary. Adjust the flavor of the sauce with the sugar if desired.

15. Spoon the sauce over the chicken and garnish with the lemon slices.

Cook's Notes

 Time
Preparation takes 40 minutes, cooking will take about 55 minutes.

 Serving Idea
Serve with rice and a green salad.

 Watchpoint
Make sure that the chicken pieces are patted dry with paper towels before you fry them or the oil will spit.

Fat Type
The chicken contains saturated fats in small amounts, the remainder is polyunsaturated fat.

SERVES 4

TROUT IN ASPIC

This attractive main course is ideal for serving as a part of a summer's meal.

7½ cups water
Pinch salt
6 black peppercorns
2 bay leaves
2 sprigs fresh parsley
1 small onion, quartered
1¼ cups dry white wine
4 even-sized rainbow trout, cleaned and well washed
2 egg whites, softly beaten
3 tbsps powdered gelatin
Lemon slices, capers and sprigs of fresh dill, to garnish

---

1. Put the water, salt, peppercorns, bay leaves, parsley, onion and wine into a large saucepan or fish kettle. Bring to the boil and simmer for about 30 minutes.

2. Cool slightly, then lay the fish into the hot stock. Cover the pan and bring back to simmering point.

3. Cook the fish gently for 5 minutes, then remove from the heat.

4. Allow the fish to cool in the covered pan before removing and draining on paper towels.

5. Reserve the stock.

6. Using a sharp knife, carefully peel away the skin from the cooked fish.

7. Using a palette knife, lift the fillets from the top of each fish, taking great care that they do not break, and lay them on a large serving dish that has a slight well in the center.

8. Lift the backbone away from the lower fillets and discard.

9. Arrange the lower fish fillets on the serving dish along with the others.

10. Strain the reserved fish stock into a large saucepan through a nylon sieve to remove the spices, herbs and vegetables.

11. Add the egg whites to the fish stock and heat gently, whipping constantly with an eggbeater.

12. While you are whipping, the egg whites should form a thick frosty crust on top which removes all particles from the stock.

13. Bring the mixture to the boil then stop whipping and allow the egg whites and liquid to rise up the sides of the pan. Remove from the heat and allow to subside. Repeat this process twice more, then allow to settle completely.

14. Line a colander with several thicknesses of paper towels or cheesecloth and stand the colander over a large bowl. Pour the fish stock into the colander along with the egg whites and allow to drain slowly. Do not allow the egg whites to fall into the clarified liquid.

15. When the liquid has drained through, remove about ½ cup and heat it gently. Sprinkle over the gelatin and allow to stand until the gelatin has dissolved completely.

16. Mix the gelatin mixture into the remaining stock and allow to cool in a refrigerator until just beginning to set.

17. Decorate the trout and the base of the dish with the lemon slices, capers and dill.

18. When the aspic has become syrupy and slightly thickened, spoon it carefully over the fish fillets for decoration.

19. Place the serving plate into a refrigerator and chill until set (about 1-2 hours).

Cook's Notes

 Time
Preparation takes 45 minutes to 1 hour. Total cooking time is about 50 minutes plus at least 1 hour to chill the dish.

! **Watchpoint**
Do not stir or whip the aspic or bubbles will form and these will spoil the appearance. For speed you can use powdered aspic, available from most delicatessens.

 Fat Type
Fish contains mono-unsaturated fats, and there are no other fats in this recipe.

SERVES 6
TURKEY KEBABS

For this low fat dish, use the ready-prepared turkey joints which are now easily available from supermarkets or butchers.

3lbs lean turkey meat
3 tsps fresh chopped sage
1 sprig rosemary, chopped
Juice 1 lemon
3 tbsps olive oil
Salt and freshly ground black pepper
¼lb lean back bacon, rind removed
Whole sage leaves

1. Remove any bone from the turkey and cut the meat into even-sized cubes.

2. Put the chopped sage, rosemary, lemon juice, oil, salt and pepper into a large bowl and stir in the turkey meat, mixing well to coat evenly. Cover and leave in the refrigerator overnight.

3. Cut the bacon strips into half lengthwise and then again crosswise.

4. Wrap these pieces around as many of the cubes of marinated turkey meat as possible.

5. Thread the turkey and bacon rolls alternately with the sage leaves and any unwrapped turkey cubes onto kebab skewers.

6. Heat the broiler to moderate, and cook the kebabs under the heat for 30 minutes, turning frequently and basting with the marinade whilst cooking. Serve immediately.

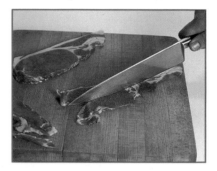

Step 3 Cut the bacon slices in half lengthwise and then again crosswise.

Step 2 Stir the cubed turkey pieces into the marinade, mixing well to coat evenly.

Step 4 Carefully roll each piece of marinated turkey in a strip of bacon.

Cook's Notes

 Time
Preparation takes 20 minutes, plus overnight soaking.
Cooking takes about 30 minutes.

 Variation
Use chicken if preferred.

 Serving Idea
Serve with pitta bread and salad, or on a bed of rice.

 Fat Type
Both chicken and turkey contain low amounts of saturated fat. The bacon contains saturated fat, but this will be reduced whilst broiling.

SERVES 6

GREEN GRAPE SHORTCAKE

Plenty of fiber in the diet will help to reduce the amount of cholesterol found in the blood, and the whole-wheat flour and grape skins in this recipe are a good source of fiber.

¼ cup polyunsaturated margarine
2 tbsps soft brown sugar
½ cup whole-wheat flour
¼ cup ground almonds
½lb green grapes, halved and pitted
2½ cups water
Thinly pared rind of 2 lemons
1½ tbsps honey
1 tbsp powdered gelatin
Few drops yellow food coloring, optional

1. Put the margarine, sugar, flour and almonds into a large bowl.

2. Work the margarine into the dry ingredients using your fingertips, and pressing the mixture together gently to form a soft dough.

3. Knead the dough lightly until it is smooth.

4. Line the base of a 8-inch loose-bottomed cake pan with silicone paper. Press the shortcake dough evenly over the base of the lined pan, making sure that it is pushed well into the sides.

5. Bake in a preheated oven 375°F for 15 minutes, or until the shortcake is firm and golden brown. Remove from the oven and allow to cool in the pan.

6. Lightly oil the inside of the cake pan above the shortcake with a little vegetable oil.

7. Arrange the grape halves on top of the shortcake.

8. Put the pint of water and lemon rind into a small pan and bring to the boil. Allow to simmer for 5 minutes, then remove the pan from the heat and allow the liquid to cool completely.

9. Strain the lemon liquid through a nylon sieve to remove the rinds. Measure off 2 cups of the strained liquid and stir in the honey.

10. Put the remaining lemon liquid into a small saucepan and heat gently until it is very hot, but not boiling.

11. Sprinkle over the gelatin and allow to stand until it has completely dissolved.

Step 7 Arrange the grape halves over the cooked shortcake whilst it is still in the pan.

12. At this stage the food coloring can be added to the liquid if desired.

13. Stir the gelatin mixture into the lemon and honey mixture and stand in a cool place until it is beginning to set.

14. Spoon the partially set jelly carefully over the grapes making sure that they remain evenly spread.

15. Stand the shortcake in a refrigerator until the jelly has set completely. Serve in wedges.

Cook's Notes

 Time
Preparation takes 45 minutes, plus cooling and chilling.
Cooking takes about 20 minutes.

 **Preparation**
It is important never to boil gelatin or it will not dissolve completely.

 Fat Type
The fat in this recipe is polyunsaturated.

SERVES 4

SPICED ORANGES WITH HONEY AND MINT

An unusual combination of flavors blend to create this light and very refreshing dessert.

1¼ cups clear honey
1½ cups water
2 large sprigs of fresh mint
12 whole cloves
4 large oranges
4 small sprigs of mint, to garnish

1. Put the honey and the water into a heavy-based saucepan. Add the mint and cloves, and slowly bring to the boil.

2. Stir the mixture to dissolve the honey and boil rapidly for 5 minutes, or until the liquid is very syrupy.

3. Cool the mixture completely, then strain the syrup through a nylon sieve into a jug or bowl to remove the sprigs of mint and cloves.

4. Using a potato peeler, carefully pare the rind very thinly from one orange.

5. Cut the pared orange rind into very fine shreds with a sharp knife.

6. Put the shreds of orange peel into a small bowl and cover with boiling water. Allow to stand until cold then drain completely, reserving only the strips of peel.

7. Stir the strips of peel into the honey syrup and chill well.

8. Peel the oranges completely, removing all the skin and especially the white pith.

Step 3 Strain the syrup through a nylon sieve into a jug or bowl to remove the sprigs of mint and cloves.

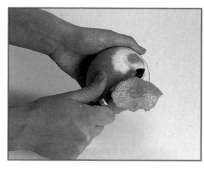

Step 4 Carefully pare the rind from one of the oranges, using a potato peeler and making sure that no white pith comes away with the rind.

9. Slice the oranges into thin rounds using a sharp knife. Arrange the orange rounds onto four individual serving plates.

10. Pour the chilled syrup over the oranges on the plates and garnish with the small sprigs of mint just before serving.

Cook's Notes

Time
Preparation takes 20 minutes, cooking takes about 5 minutes.

Fat Type
There is no fat in this recipe.

Preparation
It is important that all the white pith is removed from the oranges, otherwise this will give a bitter flavor to the dessert.

Variation
Use ruby grapefruits in place of the oranges in this recipe. Allow half a grapefruit per person, and cut it into segments rather than slices to serve.

SERVES 4-6

BRANDY SORBET WITH APPLES AND GOLDEN RAISINS

Sorbets make an ideal dessert for anyone on a low fat diet. Try this unusual combination for a real change of flavors.

2½ cups apple juice
¼ cup superfine sugar
½ cup of dried apple flakes
⅔ cup golden raisins
⅔ cup brandy
Few drops green food coloring, optional
1 egg white

1. Put the apple juice in a heavy-based saucepan along with the sugar. Heat gently, stirring until the sugar has dissolved. Bring the apple juice to the boil and boil quickly for 5 minutes. Remove from the heat and cool completely.

2. Put the apple flakes into a bowl along with the golden raisins and brandy. Add enough of the apple syrup to cover the mixture, then allow to soak for 4 hours.

3. Mix the apple flakes, golden raisins and brandy

together to form a pulp, adding the green coloring at this stage if required.

4. Whip the apple pulp into the remaining syrup, mixing thoroughly to blend evenly.

5. Pour the apple mixture into a shallow container and freeze for 2 hours or until just beginning to set.

6. Break up the partially frozen ice using a fork or electric whisk, then return to the freezer tray and continue to freeze for another hour.

7. Break up the ice crystals again, but this time mash thoroughly until they form a thick slush.

8. Whip the egg white until it is stiff, then quickly fold into the ice slush. Return to the freezer tray and freeze until completely solid.

9. Allow the ice to soften for 15 minutes before spooning into individual glass dishes.

Step 3 Beat the apple and golden raisin mixture with a fork until it becomes a thick purée.

Step 8 Fold the whipped egg whites carefully into the slushy ice before freezing completely.

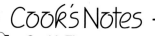 Cook's Notes

Time
Preparation takes 10 minutes, plus the soaking and freezing time.

Cook's Tip
 Use 1 cup of apple purée in place of the apple flakes and reduce the amount of apple juice used to 2 cups.

Variation
Omit the brandy from this recipe and replace with more apple juice.

Fat Type
 There is no fat of any kind in this recipe.

SERVES 6

PLUM AND HONEY COBBLER

A cobbler is a traditional English dessert, so called because of the scones which decorate the top are reminiscent of the cobbles found on old roads.

2lbs ripe plums, halved and pitted
6-9 tbsps clear honey
2 cups whole-wheat all-purpose flour
3 tbsps superfine sugar
¼ cup polyunsaturated margarine
7-9 tbsps skim milk
1 egg, beaten

1. Put the plums into an ovenproof dish along with the honey. Cover with a sheet of foil and cook in a preheated oven 400°F for 20 minutes.

2. After this time the plums should be soft and a certain amount of juice should have formed in the dish. Remove from the oven and cool completely.

3. Put the flour and the sugar into a large bowl and using your fingers, rub in the margarine until the mixture resembles fine breadcrumbs.

4. Using a round bladed knife, stir in the milk and eggs, so that the mixture forms a soft dough.

5. Turn the dough out onto a lightly floured work surface and knead it until it is smooth.

6. Roll the dough out until it is about ½-inch thick.

7. Cut the dough into rounds using a 2-inch cutter to form the cobbles.

8. Carefully arrange the scone cobbles in a circle around

Step 4 Mix the milk and egg into the flour using a round bladed knife, and pressing all ingredients together to form a soft dough.

Step 8 Arrange a circle of scone cobbles around the top edge of the dish, overlapping each one slightly.

the top edge of the dish of plums, overlapping each scone slightly.

9. Brush the top of each scone with a little milk and sprinkle with a little extra sugar. Return the plum cobbler to the oven, set at the same temperature as before, and cook until the scones are firm, risen and well browned.

10. Serve hot.

— Cook's Notes —

Time
Preparation takes 30 minutes, cooking takes 45 minutes.

Variation
Use any variation of fresh fruit in place of the plums.

Serving Idea
This dessert is delicious hot with a scoop of vanilla ice cream, but do check the fat content of the ice cream first.

Fat Type
The fats used in recipe are polyunsaturated.

SERVES 6

PEARS IN RED WINE

A delicious way of serving whole fresh pears, this dessert looks especially impressive served in glass dishes.

2½ cups dry red wine
Juice of half a lemon
1 strip lemon peel
1¼ cups sugar
1 small piece cinnamon stick
6 pears, ripe but firm
1½ tbsps slivered almonds

1. Put the wine, lemon juice, peel, sugar and cinnamon into a large deep saucepan and bring to the boil, stirring until the sugar dissolves.

2. Allow to boil rapidly for 1 minute.

3. Carefully peel the pears lengthwise and remove the small eye from the base of each pear. Leave any stalk which may be at the top intact.

4. Place the peeled pears upright in the boiled wine mixture.

5. Return the pan to the heat, bring to the boil, then simmer very gently for 20 minutes, or until the pears are soft but not mushy. Allow the pears to cool in the syrup until lukewarm, then remove and arrange in a serving dish.

6. Strain the syrup through a nylon sieve to remove the lemon peel and spices.

7. Return the syrup to the saucepan and boil rapidly until it becomes thicker and syrupy.

8. Cool the syrup completely before spooning it carefully over the pears in the serving dish.

9. Before serving, sprinkle with the slivered almonds.

Step 3 Peel the pears lengthwise and carefully remove the eye from the base of each one.

Step 4 Stand the pears in the saucepan of wine syrup; if it is possible to stand them upright and still have them covered by the sauce, then do so.

Step 5 The pears are cooked when they are soft, but not mushy and they are an even red color all over.

Cook's Notes

Time
Preparation takes 25 minutes, cooking takes 30 minutes.

Preparation
If the syrup does not completely cover the pears in the saucepan, allow them to cook on their side, but make sure they are turned frequently and basted, to ensure an even color.

Variation
Use white wine in place of the red wine in this recipe.

Fat Type
There is no fat in this recipe.

SERVES 6

CARIBBEAN FRUIT SALAD

This fruit salad is made from a refreshing mixture of tropical fruits, all of which are now easily available in most supermarkets.

½ cantaloup or honeydew melon, seeds removed
½ small pineapple
¼lb fresh strawberries
1 mango
½lb watermelon
¼lb guava
2 oranges
½ cup superfine sugar
⅔ cup white wine
Grated rind and juice of 1 lemon

1. Using a melon baller or teaspoon, scoop out rounds of flesh from the cantaloup or honeydew melon.

2. Cut the piece of pineapple in half lengthwise and carefully peel away the outer skin.

3. Remove any eyes left in the outside edge of the pineapple using a potato peeler.

4. Cut away the core from the pineapple with a serrated knife and slice the flesh thinly. Put the slices of pineapple into a large bowl along with the melon rounds.

5. Hull the strawberries and halve them. Add them to the bowl with the pineapple and melon.

6. Peel the mango, and carefully cut the flesh away from the long stone in the center of the fruit. Slice the flesh lengthwise, and stir it into the bowl of fruit.

7. Peel the watermelon and guavas, then cube the flesh. Stir these into the bowl of fruit.

8. Remove the rind from the oranges using a serrated knife. Take care to remove all the white pith, or this will flavor the fruit salad.

9. Cut the orange into segments, carefully removing the inner membrane from the segments as you slice.

10. Put the sugar, wine, lemon juice and rind into a small saucepan and warm through gently, stirring all the time until the sugar has dissolved. Do not boil, then set aside to cool.

11. Put the syrup into the bowl along with the fruit and mix thoroughly. Chill the fruit salad completely before serving.

Step 3 Remove any eyes which remain in the pineapple flesh with the pointed end of a potato peeler.

Step 6 Carefully cut the flesh away from the long inner stone of the mango, before slicing it lengthwise.

Cook's Notes

Time
Preparation takes 45 minutes, cooking takes about 3 minutes.

Preparation
It is unnecessary to remove the pips from the watermelon unless you particularly dislike them.

Watchpoint
Do not boil the syrup otherwise the flavor of the wine will be reduced.

Fat Type
There are no fats at all in this recipe.

HEALTHY COOKING

LOW
SALT

FOR A FITTER BODY

Introduction

The mineral sodium chloride, or salt, has been used over the centuries for its medicinal properties as well as its flavoring and preserving qualities. Why then should we want a low salt diet? To answer this we must look more closely at the need for and the use of salt by our bodies.

Salt is essential to the balance of acids in the blood and the maintenance of the fluid content of our cells. Without a certain amount of salt we would suffer from severe muscular cramps and bodily degeneration. The quantity that our bodies require, however, is actually very small and is easily obtainable from the whole, fresh foods we eat daily without the need to add more.

The correct balance of salt in the body is maintained by the kidneys, which remove excess salt. Too great a salt intake can lead to fluid retention, places a strain on the kidneys and can even lead to problems such as depression.

More commonly, though, high sodium levels in the body can be directly linked to abnormally high blood pressure, or hypertension. All Western countries with a high salt consumption have a problem with high blood pressure. This, along with obesity and smoking, has been found to be one of the major causes of fatal heart disease.

Unfortunately, the taste for salt is addictive and people tend to feel that their bodies require large amounts. Whilst this may be true in a few instances, under normal conditions this is simply not the case. People simply become accustomed to the excessive use of salt and feel that without it their food lacks taste. Gradually their bodies remove less of the excess sodium, and problems begin.

In this book, the recipes rely on alternative flavorings to enhance the taste of food. These ingredients may not have been available in ancient times when the taste for salt was established, but they are now easy to obtain. The recipes are simple to prepare and show just how easily you can adapt to a pattern of eating that will, with time, reduce your need for the flavor of salt.

MAKES 24

MAKES 24

AVOCADO CHEESE SNACKS

A delightful combination of avocado, nuts and cheese, this recipe doesn't need the addition of salt to enhance the taste of these delicious party snacks.

1 ripe avocado
2½ tbsps light cream or natural yogurt
1 clove garlic, minced
1¼ tsps lemon juice
¾ cup finely grated Cheddar cheese
1¼ tsps ready-made English mustard
½ cup fresh white breadcrumbs
3 green onions, finely chopped
Freshly ground black pepper, to taste
2½ tbsps freshly chopped parsley
⅓ cup toasted, chopped almonds

Step 5 Form teaspoonfuls of the avocado mixture into small balls using your hands.

Step 7 Roll each ball into the finely chopped parsley, coating them thoroughly.

Step 1 After cutting, carefully twist the avocado apart to make two halves.

1. Cut the avocado in half lengthwise and carefully twist it apart.

2. Remove the stone and peel away the skin from the avocado halves using a sharp knife.

3. Mash the avocado flesh into a medium-sized bowl using a fork or a small potato masher.

4. Stir the cream or yogurt, garlic, lemon juice, grated cheese, mustard, breadcrumbs, onions and pepper into the mashed avocado. Mix together well with a fork until a stiff paste results.

5. Using your hands, roll teaspoonfuls of the avocado mixture into small balls.

6. Spread the parsley onto one small plate and the almonds onto another.

7. Roll half the number of avocado balls into the finely chopped parsley pressing it gently into the surface to coat thoroughly.

8. Roll the remaining avocado balls into the almonds in the same manner.

9. Refrigerate the coated snacks for 40 minutes before serving with drinks.

Cook's Notes

 Time
Preparation takes 30 minutes, plus 30 minutes refrigeration time.

 **Preparation**
It is most important to keep the mixture cool when preparing these snacks. If you have difficulty forming the mixture into small balls, refrigerate for at least 30 minutes.

 Variation
Use finely chopped walnuts instead of the almonds, and Stilton cheese instead of the Cheddar.

MAKES 36

STUFFED EGGS

Stuffed eggs make an attractive, and deliciously different, party appetizer.

18 small eggs, or quail eggs
¼ cup unsalted butter
1 clove garlic, minced
½ cup cooked, peeled shrimp, finely chopped
¾ tsp finely chopped fresh basil
Freshly ground black pepper, to taste

1. Cook the eggs in boiling water for 5 minutes. Drain, and plunge them immediately into cold water.

2. Allow the eggs to cool completely, then remove the shells. Rinse and drain.

3. Cut each egg in half lengthwise and carefully remove the yolks.

4. Put the yolks into a large bowl and beat in the butter and garlic. Mix well.

5. Add the shrimp, basil and pepper to the creamed egg

yolk mixture. Beat thoroughly until a soft consistency results.

6. Fill each egg white half with a little of the prepared mixture, piling it attractively into the cavity left by the egg yolk.

7. Refrigerate until required.

Step 3 Using a sharp knife, halve the hard-cooked eggs lengthwise.

Step 4 Cream the butter and garlic into the egg yolks, beating thoroughly to mix well.

Step 6 Pile equal amounts of the filling mixture into the halved egg whites, forking it attractively to serve.

Cook's Notes

Time
Preparation takes 15 minutes, cooking takes 5 minutes.

Variation
Use flaked white crab meat instead of the shrimp.
For a more exotic dish, use quails' eggs instead of hens' eggs.

Serving Idea
Serve the filled egg halves on a plate which has been garnished with lettuce leaves and tiny pieces of red pepper.

MAKES 12oz

SPICED NUTS

Everyone likes to nibble nuts with drinks at a party, but most contain very high quantities of salt. These delicious spiced nuts contain no salt, are extremely easy to make, and can be prepared well in advance.

2½ tbsps corn or vegetable oil
1 cup fresh peanuts, shelled and husked
1 cup blanched almonds
1 cup fresh cashew nuts, shelled and husked
¾ tsp ground ginger
¾ tsps ground cinnamon
¾ tsp cayenne pepper

1. Heat the oil in a large frying pan.

Step 2 Stir the nuts into the hot oil, making sure they are evenly coated.

2. Stir in the nuts, mixing well to coat evenly with the hot oil.

3. Sprinkle the spices over the nuts and stir well to coat evenly.

4. Transfer the nuts to an ovenproof dish, spreading them

Step 3 Sprinkle the spices over the nuts and mix well.

Step 4 Spread the nuts in an even layer on an ovenproof baking dish.

in an even layer.

5. Toast the nuts for 10-15 minutes in a preheated oven, 375°F.

6. To prevent the nuts from burning, turn them once or twice during the cooking time.

Cook's Notes

Time
Preparation takes 10 minutes, cooking takes 10-15 minutes.

Cook's Tip
Prepare these nuts in advance and store them for up to 2 weeks in an airtight container.

Variation
Use hazelnuts instead of cashew nuts, and ground cardamom, cumin and chili powder instead of the ginger, cinnamon and cayenne pepper.

SERVES 4-6

SPICY CHILI

This "complete meal" dish certainly doesn't need salt to bring out the full flavor of the ingredients.

3¾ tbsps vegetable oil
2 onions, roughly chopped
1 clove garlic, minced
1¼ tbsps ground cumin
2½ tsps ground paprika
1 red or green chili pepper, seeded and finely chopped
½lb ground beef
1¾lbs canned tomatoes, chopped
3¾ cups chicken or vegetable stock
⅓ cup tomato paste
1¼ tsps oregano
1 bay leaf
⅔ cup beer
Freshly ground black pepper
½ cup each of canned red kidney beans, chick peas, and white pinto beans, drained and thoroughly rinsed.

1. Heat the oil in a large, heavy-based saucepan.

2. Add the onion and garlic and cook slowly until they become transparent.

3. Stir in the cumin, paprika and chili pepper. Increase the heat and cook quickly for 30 seconds, stirring all the time.

4. Add the meat and cook until lightly browned, breaking up any large pieces with a fork.

5. Add the tomatoes and their juice, the stock, tomato paste, oregano, bay leaf, beer and ground pepper. Stir well, then bring to the boil.

6. Cover and simmer for approximately 50 minutes, checking the level of liquid several times during the cooking and adding more water if the soup seems too dry.

7. During the last 15 minutes of cooking, add the drained beans, stirring them in to mix well.

Step 4 Add the meat and cook until lightly browned, breaking up any large pieces with a fork.

Step 7 Add the drained beans during the last 15 minutes of cooking time.

Cook's Notes

Time
Preparation takes 30 minutes, cooking takes 1 hour.

Freezing
This soup freezes well.

Cook's Tip
If you cannot buy canned beans and chick peas, use 2oz each of dried beans. Soak them overnight and cook thoroughly for 1 hour before using in this recipe.

Serving Idea
Serve with a mixed garnish of chopped fresh tomatoes, chopped green onions and cubed avocado which has been sprinkled with lemon juice.

SERVES 4-6

ZUCCHINI SOUP

The fresh taste of lemon and zucchini makes a delicious soup which can be served either hot or cold.

1 medium-sized onion, thinly sliced
2½ tbsps olive oil
1lb zucchini, topped, tailed and sliced
Finely grated rind and juice of 1 large lemon
1¾ cups chicken stock
Freshly ground black pepper
2 egg yolks
¾ cup natural yogurt

1. In a large pan, fry the onion gently in the olive oil for 3 minutes until it is just transparent.

2. Add the zucchini and fry for a further 2-3 minutes.

Step 1 In a large pan, gently fry the onion until it is just transparent.

3. Stir in all remaining ingredients except the egg yolks and yogurt, cover and simmer for 20 minutes.

4. Transfer the soup to a liquidizer or food processor, and blend until smooth.

Step 4 Blend the soup in a liquidizer, or food processor, until it is smooth.

Step 5 Mix together the egg yolks and yogurt in a small jug or bowl.

5. Mix the egg yolks into the yogurt and stir into the blended soup.

6. Reheat the soup gently, stirring all the time until it thickens.

7. Serve hot at this stage, or transfer to a refrigerator and chill thoroughly.

Cook's Notes

 Time
Preparation takes 20 minutes, plus chiling time, cooking takes 25 minutes.

 Serving Idea
Serve the soup with a garnish of thinly sliced zucchini and light French toasts.

Preparation
Great care must be taken not to boil the soup once the egg yolks have been added, otherwise the mixture will curdle.

 **Freezing**
This soup can be frozen, but not after the egg yolks have been added. Freeze before this stage, defrost and then finish the recipe as described.

SERVES 4
SEVICHE

*In this traditional Mexican dish the raw fish is "cooked" in a mixture of oil
and lime juice. Quick and easy to prepare, seviche makes
a highly nutritious and very tasty appetizer.*

1lb fresh cod fillet
Juice and grated rind of 2 limes
1 small shallot, finely chopped
1 green chili pepper, seeded and finely chopped
1¼ tsps ground coriander
1 small green pepper, seeded and sliced
1 small red pepper, seeded and sliced
1¼ tbsps freshly chopped parsley
1¼ tbsps freshly chopped coriander
4 green onions, finely chopped
2½ tbsps olive oil
Freshly ground black pepper
1 small lettuce, to serve

1. Carefully remove the skin from the cod fillets.

2. Using a sharp knife cut the fish into very thin strips across the grain.

3. Put the fish strips into a large bowl and pour over the lime juice.

4. Stir in the grated lime rind, shallot, chili pepper and ground coriander. Mix well.

5. Cover the bowl with plastic wrap or a damp cloth and refrigerate for 24 hours, stirring occasionally during this time to ensure that the fish remains well coated in the lime.

6. Mix the sliced peppers, green onions and the fresh herbs together in a large bowl.

7. Put the fish mixture into a colander and drain off the juice.

8. Put the drained fish into the pepper mixture and stir in the oil, mixing well to coat evenly. Add freshly ground pepper to taste.

9. Finely shred the lettuce and arrange on a serving plate.

10. Spread the fish mixture attractively over the lettuce and serve immediately, garnished with slices of lime, if liked.

Step 2 Cut the cod fillet across the grain into very thin slices.

Step 1 Using a sharp knife, carefully remove the skin from the cod fillets.

Step 5 After refrigerating for 24 hours, the fish should have a cooked appearance.

Cook's Notes

Time
Preparation takes 20 minutes, plus 24 hours standing time.

Variation
Use hake or salmon in place of the cod in this recipe.

Serving Idea
As well as being an interesting appetizer, Seviche can also be served with pitta breads for a tasty lunch.

SERVES 6-8

Spinach-Chicken Pâté

*This superb pâté is ideal when you want to impress your guests
with a delicious appetizer.*

½lb chicken breasts, boned and skinned
2 egg whites
2 cups fresh white breadcrumbs
1lb fresh spinach, washed
1¼ tbsps each of fresh finely chopped chervil, chives and tarragon
Freshly ground black pepper
1¼ cups heavy cream
⅓ cup finely chopped walnuts
Pinch nutmeg

Step 4 The spinach should be cooked until it is just wilted, using only the water that clings to the leaves and adding no extra liquid.

1. Cut the chicken into small pieces.

2. Put the cut chicken, 1 egg white and half of the breadcrumbs into a food processor. Blend until well mixed.

3. Put the spinach into a large saucepan and cover with a tight-fitting lid.

4. Cook the spinach for 3 minutes, or until it has just wilted.

5. Remove the chicken mixture from the food processor and rinse the bowl.

6. Put the spinach into the food processor along with the herbs, the remaining egg white and breadcrumbs. Blend until smooth.

7. Season the chicken mixture with a little pepper and add half of the cream. Mix well to blend thoroughly.

8. Add the remaining cream to the spinach along with the walnuts and the nutmeg. Beat this mixture well to blend thoroughly.

9. Line a 1lb loaf pan with wax paper. Lightly oil this with a little vegetable oil.

10. Pour the chicken mixture into the base of the pan and spread evenly.

11. Carefully pour the spinach mixture over the chicken mixture, and smooth the top with a palette knife.

12. Cover the pan with lightly oiled aluminum foil and seal this tightly around the edges.

13. Stand the pan in a roasting dish and pour enough warm water into the dish to come halfway up the sides of the pan.

14. Cook the pâté in a preheated oven 325°F for 1 hour, or until it is firm.

15. Put the pâté into the refrigerator and chill for at least 12 hours.

16. Carefully lift the pâté out of the pan and peel off the paper. To serve, cut the pâté into thin slices with a sharp knife.

Cook's Notes

Time
Preparation takes 25 minutes, cooking takes 1 hour.

Serving Idea
Serve slices of the terrine on individual serving plates garnished with a little salad.

Watchpoint
Do not overcook the terrine or attempt to cook it any more quickly than the recipe states, otherwise it will curdle and spoil.

SERVES 4

SPANISH EGGPLANTS

This delicious eggplant dish is highly reminiscent of Andalucia in Spain where tomatoes, rice and tuna fish are very popular ingredients.

4 small eggplants
3¾ tbsps olive oil
1 small onion, finely chopped
1 clove garlic, minced
¾ cup cooked whole grain rice
7oz can tuna in oil, drained and fish coarsely flaked
1¼ tbsps mayonnaise
1¼ tsps curry powder
4 fresh tomatoes, skinned, seeded and chopped
1 tbsp coarsely chopped parsley
Freshly ground black pepper

1. Cut the eggplants in half lengthwise. Score the cut surfaces lightly with a sharp knife at regular intervals.

2. Brush the scored surface lightly with 1 tbsp of the olive oil and place the eggplants on a greased baking dish.

3. Bake the eggplants in a preheated oven 375°F, for 15 minutes, or until beginning to soften.

4. Cool the eggplants slightly, then carefully scoop the center flesh from each half. Take care that you do not break the skin at this stage.

5. Fry the chopped onion gently in the remaining olive oil for 3 minutes, or until they are just transparent.

6. Add the garlic and the eggplant flesh, and fry for a further 2 minutes. Season to taste with pepper.

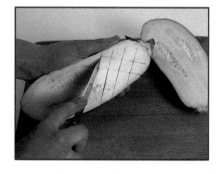

Step 1 Taking care not to break the skins, score the cut surface of the eggplant halves at regular intervals with a sharp, pointed knife.

Step 4 Cool the eggplants slightly, then carefully scoop the center flesh from each half. Take care that you do not break the skin at this stage.

7. Add the rice, flaked tuna, mayonnaise, curry powder, tomatoes, parsley and black pepper to the eggplant mixture, and mix together well.

8. Pile equal amounts of this rice and tuna filling into the eggplant shells. Return the filled eggplants to the ovenproof baking dish. Brush with the remaining olive oil, and bake in the oven for a further 25 minutes. Serve piping hot.

Cook's Notes

 Time
Preparation will take 40 minutes, cooking takes about 50 minutes.

 Serving Idea
Serve with a crisp mixed-leaf salad and black olives.

 **Preparation**
Use a serrated grapefruit knife to remove the baked eggplant flesh without tearing the skins.

 Variation
For a tasty vegetarian variation, use 6oz button mushrooms in place of the tuna.

MAKES 1

HAM AND GREEN PEPPER OMELET

Use "tendersweet" ham in this recipe to keep the salt content as low as possible.

3 eggs
2½ tbsps milk
Freshly ground black pepper
1¼ tbsps vegetable oil
¼ cup chopped green pepper
2 tomatoes, peeled, seeded and roughly chopped
2oz lean ham, cut into small dice

1. Break the eggs into the bowl and beat in the milk and pepper.

2. Heat the oil in a omelet pan and fry the green pepper until it is just soft.

3. Stir in the tomatoes and the ham. Heat through for 1 minute.

4. Pour the egg mixture into the frying pan over the vegetables. Stir the mixture briskly with a wooden spoon, until it begins to cook.

5. As the egg begins to set, lift it slightly and tilt the pan to allow the uncooked egg underneath.

6. When the egg on top is still slightly creamy, fold the omelet in half and slip it onto a serving plate. Serve immediately

Step 5 Lift the cooked egg with a fork and tilt the frying pan to allow uncooked egg underneath.

Step 2 Gently fry the pepper in hot oil until it begins to soften.

Step 6 Fold the omelet in half whilst the top of the egg is still slightly creamy.

Cook's Notes

Time
Preparation takes about 15 minutes, cooking takes 5 minutes.

Serving Idea
Serve the omelet with a crisp leaf salad and French bread.

Cook's Tip
To peel tomatoes easily, cut a small cross into the skin and drop them into boiling water for about 10 seconds, then plunge into cold water. This loosens the peel.

Variation
Use any selection of your favorite vegetables to vary this delicious dish.

SERVES 4

STUFFED TOMATOES

Fresh herbs complement the sweetness of tomatoes, making the addition of salt unnecessary.

4 large ripe tomatoes
2½ tbsps olive oil
1 clove garlic, minced
2x½-inch-thick slices white bread, crusts removed
1¼ tbsps chopped parsley
2½ tsps chopped thyme or marjoram
Freshly ground black pepper

Step 1 Using a grapefruit knife, carefully scoop the flesh out of each tomato half, making sure that you do not break the shells.

1. Cut the tomatoes in half and carefully cut out the tomato pulp using a grapefruit knife.

2. Put the tomato pulp into a sieve and press out the juice using the back of a wooden spoon. Put the dry tomato pulp into a large bowl.

3. Mix the olive oil and garlic together. Brush both sides of the bread with this mixture and leave to stand for 10 minutes.

4. Using a sharp knife, chop the oiled bread and the herbs together until they are well mixed and fine textured.

Stir this into the tomato pulp and add black pepper.

5. Press the tomato filling into the tomato shells, piling it slightly above the cut edge.

Step 2 Put the tomato pulp into a sieve and press out as much juice as possible using the back of a wooden spoon.

Step 4 Using a sharp knife, chop the herbs and the oiled bread together until they are as fine as breadcrumbs.

6. Arrange the tomatoes on an ovenproof dish and broil under a low heat for 5 minutes.

7. Raise the temperature of the broiler to high and brown the tomatoes on top for a few seconds. Serve at once.

Cook's Notes

Time
Preparation takes 15-20 minutes. Cooking time takes 5 minutes.

Cook's Tip
Prepare the tomatoes in advance and broil them just before serving.

Serving Idea
Serve with a rice salad for a light lunch.

102

SERVES 4-6

MUSHROOM SALAD

Mushrooms have a flavor all of their own and do not require salt.
This salad can be made using cultivated
mushrooms, but it is extra special when prepared with wild ones.

1lb button or oyster mushrooms
1 medium-sized onion
3¾ tbsps vegetable oil
1¼ tbsps freshly chopped parsley
1 cucumber, finely diced
3-4 tomatoes, peeled, seeded and sliced
5 tbsps olive oil
1¼ tbsps white wine vinegar
Freshly ground black pepper
1 small iceberg lettuce

1. Trim the mushrooms and rub clean with a damp cloth.

2. Slice the mushrooms very thinly and chop the onions finely.

Step 2 Slice the mushrooms very thinly with a sharp knife.

3. Heat the vegetable oil in a large frying pan and gently sauté the mushrooms and onions for 2-3 minutes, or until they are just soft. Allow to cool.

Step 3 Fry the mushrooms and onions gently in hot oil until they just begin to soften.

Step 4 Add the parsley, cucumber and tomatoes to the mushrooms, mixing well to combine ingredients evenly.

4. When the mushrooms have cooled, stir in the parsley, cucumber and tomatoes.

5. Mix together the oil, vinegar and pepper in a small jug, and pour over all the other ingredients.

6. Stir gently to coat evenly, and refrigerate for 1-2 hours.

7. Shred the lettuce finely and arrange on a serving plate. Spread the chilled mushrooms evenly over the lettuce.

Cook's Notes

Time
Preparation takes 10 minutes, cooking takes 5 minutes.
Chiling time is a minimum of 2 hours.

Cook's Tip
The salad can be prepared a day in advance and stored in the refrigerator until required.

Serving Ideas
Serve with Melba toast or crusty whole-wheat rolls.

SERVES 4

CHINESE MEATBALLS

The spicy nature of this dish means that there is no need to add salt.

¾ cup blanched almonds
1lb ground beef
1¼ tsps grated fresh ginger
1 clove garlic, minced
½ large green pepper, seeded and chopped
Dash of Szechwan, chili, or Tabasco sauce
2½ tbsps soy sauce
Oil for frying
3¾ tbsps soy sauce
¼ cup vegetable stock
1¼ tbsps rice wine or white wine vinegar
2½ tsps honey
1¼ tbsps sherry
1¼ tbsps cornstarch
4 green onions, sliced diagonally

your hands to ensure that the ingredients are well blended.

4. Divide the mixture into16 and roll each piece into small meatballs on a lightly floured board.

5. Heat a little oil in a large frying pan and lay in about half of the meatballs in a single layer.

6. Cook the meatballs over a low heat for about 20 minutes, turning them frequently until they are well browned all over.

7. Transfer to a serving dish and keep warm while you cook the remaining meatballs. Set aside as before.

8. Stir the 3¾ tbsps soy sauce, stock and vinegar into the frying pan and bring to the boil. Boil briskly for about 30 seconds.

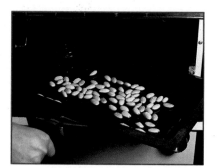

Step 1 Toast the almonds gently under a broiler until pale gold in color, stirring them frequently to prevent them from burning.

Step 6 Gently fry the meatballs in the hot oil until they are evenly browned.

1. Spread the almonds evenly onto a broiler pan, and broil under a low heat for 3-4 minutes, or until lightly toasted. Stir the almonds often to prevent them from burning.

2. Chop the almonds coarsely using a large sharp knife.

3. In a large bowl, combine the chopped almonds with the meat, ginger, garlic, green pepper, Szechwan sauce, and the 2½ tbsps of soy sauce. Use a wooden spoon or

9. Add the honey and stir until dissolved.

10. Blend the sherry and cornstarch together in a small bowl, and add this into the hot sauce. Cook, stirring all the time, until thickened.

11. Arrange the meatballs on a serving dish and sprinkle with the sliced green onions. Pour the sauce over, and serve.

Cook's Notes

Time
Preparation takes about 20 minutes, cooking takes 40 minutes.

Serving Idea
Serve with boiled rice and a tomato salad.

Freezing
The meatballs will freeze uncooked for up to 3 months. The sauce should be prepared freshly when required.

SERVES 4-6

CHICKEN CACCIATORE

The use of herbs, wine and vinegar in this delicious Italian family meal gives a wonderful, hearty flavor without the need for salt.

5 tbsps olive oil
3lbs chicken pieces
2 onions, sliced
3 cloves garlic, minced
8oz button mushrooms, quartered
½ cup red wine
1¼ tbsps wine vinegar
1¼ tbsps fresh chopped parsley
2½ tsps fresh chopped oregano
2½ tsps fresh chopped basil
1 bay leaf
1lb canned tomatoes
½ cup chicken stock
Freshly ground black pepper
Pinch of sugar

1. In a large frying pan heat the oil and lay the chicken pieces, skin side down, in one layer.

2. Brown for 3-4 minutes, then turn each piece over.

Continue turning the chicken portions until all surfaces are well browned.

3. Remove the chicken portions to a plate and keep warm.

4. Add the onions and garlic to the oil and chicken juices in the frying pan. Cook lightly for 2-3 minutes, or until they are just beginning to brown.

5. Add the mushrooms to the pan and cook for about 1 minute, stirring constantly.

6. Pour the wine and vinegar into the pan and boil rapidly to reduce to about half the original quantity.

7. Add the herbs, bay leaf and tomatoes, stirring well to break up the tomatoes.

8. Stir in the chicken stock and season with pepper and sugar.

9. Return the chicken to the tomato sauce and cover with a tight-fitting lid. Simmer for about 1 hour, or until the chicken is tender.

Step 2 Turn the chicken frequently until all the outer surfaces are golden brown.

Step 7 Break the tomatoes in the pan by pressing them gently with the back of a wooden spoon.

Cook's Notes

Time
Preparation takes about 20 minutes, cooking takes 1 hour 15 minutes.

Serving Idea
Serve with rice or pasta, and a mixed salad.

Variation
Use the delicious sauce in this recipe with any other meat of your choice.

Freezing
This dish freezes well for up to 3 months. Defrost thoroughly and reheat by simmering for at least 30 minutes before serving.

SERVES 4

HERBED HERRINGS

The fresh taste of dill and mild mustard is all that is required to bring out the full flavor of fresh herring.

5 tbsps fresh chopped dill
7½ tbsps mild mustard
2½ tbsps lemon juice or white wine
4-8 fresh herrings, cleaned, but heads and tails left on
2½ tbsps unsalted butter, melted
Freshly ground black pepper
Lemon wedges and whole sprigs of fresh dill, to garnish

Step 2 Using a very sharp knife, cut 3 shallow slits just through the skin on each side of the fish.

Step 1 Mix the dill, mustard and lemon juice or white wine together in a small bowl, mixing well to blend all these ingredients thoroughly.

Step 3 Spread the mustard mixture over each fish, carefully pushing a little into each cut.

1. Put the dill, mustard and lemon juice or white wine into a small bowl and mix together thoroughly.

2. Using a sharp knife, cut three shallow slits through the skin on both sides of each fish.

3. Spread half of the mustard mixture over one side of each fish, pushing some of the mixture into each cut.

4. Drizzle a little of the melted butter over the fish and broil under a preheated broiler for 5-6 minutes.

5. Using a fish slice, carefully turn each fish over, and spread with the remaining dill and mustard mixture.

6. Drizzle over the remaining butter and broil for a further 5-6 minutes, or until the fish is thoroughly cooked.

7. Sprinkle the fish with black pepper and serve garnished with the dill sprigs and lemon wedges.

Cook's Notes

Time
Preparation takes 10 minutes, cooking takes 12-15 minutes.

Cook's Tip
To be sure that the fish you are buying are completely fresh, make sure that the skins are moist and the eyes are bright.

Variation
Use mackerel instead of the herrings in this recipe.

Serving Idea
Serve with new potatoes and green vegetables.

LOW SALT

SERVES 4

SWEET AND SOUR TURKEY MEATBALLS

These easy-to-prepare turkey meatballs are served with a highly flavored sweet and sour sauce.

1 small onion, finely chopped
2½ tbsps olive oil
1lb raw turkey
1 clove garlic, minced
2½ tbsps fresh parsley, chopped
2½ tbsps blanched almonds, finely chopped
Freshly ground black pepper
Pinch mixed spice
1¼ tbsps chopped raisins
2½ tbsps fresh whole-wheat breadcrumbs
1 egg, beaten
4 green onions, thinly sliced
1¼ cups pure tomato juice
2½ tbsps tomato paste
Juice of half a lemon
1¼ tbsps honey
1 green chili, seeded and thinly sliced
2 slices fresh pineapple, finely chopped
1 medium-sized red pepper, seeded and cut into thin strips
2 carrots, peeled and coarsely grated

1. Fry the onions gently in the olive oil until they are just transparent.

2. Using a food processor or mincer, finely chop or grind the raw turkey.

3. Put the ground turkey into a large bowl, along with the garlic, parsley, almonds, pepper, mixed spice, raisins, breadcrumbs and egg.

4. Stir in the cooked onion and the oil, mixing well to combine all ingredients thoroughly.

5. Divide the mixture into 16 and shape each piece into a small ball. Chill for 30 minutes.

Step 4 Stir the fried onions and the oil into the ground turkey mixture, mixing thoroughly to ensure that all ingredients are blended evenly.

Step 5 Divide the mixture into 16 and shape each piece into a small ball using lightly floured hands.

6. Put all the remaining ingredients into a shallow pan and bring to the boil. Cover the pan and simmer the sauce gently for 10 minutes, stirring occasionally.

7. Carefully drop the chilled meatballs into the sauce. Re-cover and simmer for a further 20 minutes, or until the meatballs are completely cooked.

Cook's Notes

 Time
Preparation takes 20-25 minutes, cooking time takes about 35 minutes.

 Serving Idea
Serve with brown rice or whole-wheat pasta.

Preparation
If the sauce evaporates too quickly, add a little stock or water to keep it to a thin enough consistency.

 Cook's Tip
The shaped meatballs can be lightly fried in a little oil before being added to the sauce, if preferred.

SERVES 4

SKATE WINGS WITH BUTTER SAUCE

Fish of any kind is an excellent source of iodine for people who are on a low salt diet. Skate wings are both economical and delicious, and can make an interesting change from everyday fish dishes.

4 wings of skate
1 very small onion, sliced
2 parsley stalks
6 black peppercorns
1¼ cups vegetable or fish stock
5 tbsps unsalted butter
1¼ tbsps capers
2½ tbsps white wine vinegar
1¼ tbsps fresh chopped parsley

1. Place the skate wings in one layer in a large deep sauté pan.

2. Add the onion slices, parsley stalks and peppercorns, then pour over the stock.

3. Bring the fish gently to the boil with the pan uncovered and allow to simmer for 10-15 minutes.

4. Carefully remove the skate wings from the pan and arrange on a serving platter.

Step 1 Place the skate wings in a pan along with the onion slice, parsley stalks, peppercorns and stock.

5. Remove any skin or large pieces of bone, taking great care not the break up the fish. Keep warm.

6. Place the butter into a small pan and cook over a high heat until it begins to brown.

7. Add the capers and immediately remove the butter from the heat. Stir in the vinegar to foam the hot butter.

8. Pour the hot butter sauce over the skate wings and sprinkle with some chopped parsley. Serve immediately.

Step 5 Carefully remove any skin or large bones from the cooked fish using a small sharp pointed knife.

Step 7 Add the vinegar to the hot butter and capers. This will cause the butter to froth.

Cook's Notes

Time
Preparation takes10-15 minutes, cooking will take 20 minutes.

Serving Idea
Serve with fresh vegetables and new or jacket potatoes.

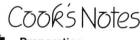

Preparation
When the skate is completely cooked, the meat will pull away from the bones in long strips.

Watchpoint
Take care not to burn the butter when heating it rapidly. It should only just begin to brown, before adding the capers and vinegar.

SERVES 4

CHICKEN WITH APPLE CREAM SAUCE

Fresh tasting apples and tender chicken make this low salt recipe ideal for serving as part of a special meal.

¼ cup unsalted butter
2½ tbsps vegetable oil
8 skinned and boned chicken breasts
5 tbsps brandy
2 dessert apples, peeled, cored and coarsely chopped
1 shallot, finely chopped
2 sticks celery, finely chopped
¾ tsp dried thyme, crumbled
7½ tbsps chicken stock
2 eggs, lightly beaten
7½ tbsps heavy cream

1. Melt half the butter and all of the oil in a large sauté pan until it is foaming.

2. Add the chicken and fry gently, turning once or twice, until each piece is well browned.

3. Pour off most of the fat from the pan, leaving just the chicken pieces and their juices to cook.

4. Pour the brandy into the pan with the chicken and heat gently. Carefully ignite the brandy with a match and shake the sauté pan until the flames subside.

5. In a small saucepan or frying pan, melt the remaining butter. Stir in the chopped apple, shallot and celery. Cook for about 5 minutes, until soft, but not brown.

6. Add the cooked apples to the chicken portions, along with the thyme and stock. Bring the chicken to the boil, cover, reduce the heat and simmer for 30 minutes.

7. Remove the chicken from the pan and arrange on a serving dish. Put the eggs and cream into a bowl and gradually whip in some of the hot sauce from the sauté pan. Continue whipping until all the hot sauce has been added and the mixture is smooth.

8. Return the sauce to the sauté pan and heat gently over a low temperature for 2-3 minutes, stirring constantly until the sauce thickens. Pour the hot sauce over the chicken breasts and serve garnished with some watercress.

Step 4 Carefully ignite the warmed brandy, shaking the pan gently until the flames subside.

Step 7 Whipping vigorously with an eggbeater, gradually add the hot sauce mixture to the eggs and cream, beating until smooth.

Cook's Notes

Time
Preparation takes 25-30 minutes, cooking takes 40-50 minutes.

Preparation
If preferred, the sauce can be blended using a food processor or liquidiser instead of whipping by hand.

Serving Idea
Serve with sauté potatoes and petit pois.

Watchpoint
Take great care not to allow the sauce to boil once the egg and cream is added or it will curdle.

SERVES 4

MEDITERRANEAN SHELLFISH CASSEROLE

Fresh shellfish cooked with red wine and tomatoes makes an impressive main course to serve for that special dinner party.

1 onion, peeled and finely chopped
2 cloves garlic, minced
3¾ tbsps olive oil
1½lbs tomatoes, skinned, seeded and chopped
2½ tbsps tomato paste
2½ cups dry red wine
Freshly ground black pepper
1 quart mussels, in their shells
8 large Mediterranean shrimp, in their shells
⅔ cup peeled shrimp
⅔ cup white crab meat
8 small crab claws, for garnish
2½ tbsps vegetable oil
1 clove garlic, minced
1 tbsp fresh chopped parsley
8 slices stale French bread

1. In a large saucepan, fry the onion gently in the olive oil for 3 minutes, or until transparent but not browned.

2. Add the 2 cloves of garlic and chopped tomatoes to the onions, fry gently for a further 3 minutes, stirring to break up the tomatoes.

3. Stir in the tomato paste, red wine and black pepper. Bring the sauce to the boil; cover and simmer for 15 minutes.

4. Scrub the mussels to remove any small barnacles or bits of seaweed attached to the shells.

5. If any of the mussels are open, tap them gently with the handle of a knife. If they do not close up immediately, discard.

6. Drop all tightly closed mussels into the simmering tomato sauce. Cover and cook for 5 minutes.

Step 4 Trim any small barnacles or pieces of seaweed away from the mussel shells using a small, sharp knife.

Step 6 After cooking for 5 minutes in the tomato sauce, all the mussels should have opened completely. Any that do not, must be removed and discarded.

7. Add the whole shrimp, peeled shrimp, crab and claws to the mussels and tomatoes. Re-cover and simmer for 5 minutes.

8. Heat the vegetable oil in a frying pan and stir in the remaining garlic clove and parsley.

9. Put the slices of French bread into the hot oil and fry until brown on one side. Turn each slice over and fry until the second side is well browned.

10. Spoon the fish stew into a deep sided serving dish and arrange the garlic croutons over the top. Stir briefly before serving.

Cook's Notes

Time
Preparation takes 15-20 minutes, cooking takes about 30 minutes.

Preparation
All the mussels must have opened completely after being cooked in the tomato sauce. Any that do not, must be removed and discarded.

Serving Idea
Serve with a large mixed salad and perhaps some extra French bread to mop up the sauce.

SERVES 6

STUFFED VEAL

*Sorrel gives this dish a unique flavor. If sorrel is unavailable,
use fresh spinach instead.*

2lbs rolled roast of veal
½ cup garlic cheese spread
4oz sorrel leaf, finely chopped
2½ tsps fresh oregano or marjoram, chopped
½ cup finely chopped walnuts
Freshly ground black pepper
½ cup all-purpose flour
⅔ tsp paprika
1 egg, beaten
1 cup dried breadcrumbs
3¾ tbsps unsalted butter, melted

Step 2 Spread the filling ingredients evenly over the inside of the meat.

1. Unroll the veal roast and trim off some of the fat from the outside using a sharp knife.

2. Put the cheese, sorrel, oregano or marjoram, walnuts and black pepper into a bowl. Mix together using a round bladed knife or your hands, until the ingredients are well bound together. Spread this filling over the inside of the veal.

3. Roll the veal roast up, jelly-roll fashion, and sew the ends together with a trussing needle and thick thread.

4. Dredge the veal roll with the flour and sprinkle with the paprika. Press this coating well onto the meat using your hands.

5. Brush the floured meat liberally with beaten egg and roll it into the dried breadcrumbs, pressing gently to make sure that all surfaces are thoroughly coated.

Step 3 Sew the ends of the joint together using a trussing needle and strong thread.

6. Place the coated veal on a cookie sheet, brush with melted butter and roast in a preheated oven 325°F, for 1 hour, or until the meat is well cooked.

7. Allow to stand for 10 minutes before slicing and serving hot, or chill and serve cold.

Cook's Notes

 Time
Preparation takes 25 minutes, cooking takes 1-1½ hours.

 Variation
Use a rolled roast of lamb instead of the veal.

 **Serving Idea**
Serve with salad or vegetables and a rich brown sauce.

 Freezing
This recipe will freeze well, and is ideal prepared in advance and served cold, after being thawed.

SERVES 4

CORNISH GAME HEN WITH SPICY SAUCE

Although this recipe takes quite a while to prepare, the end result will make your effort worthwhile.

4 Cornish game hens
1¼ tsps each of paprika, mustard powder and ground ginger
¾ tsp ground turmeric
Pinch ground allspice
5 tbsps unsalted butter
2½ tbsps chili sauce
1¼ tbsps plum chutney
1¼ tbsps brown sauce
1¼ tbsps Worcestershire sauce
1¼ tbsps soy sauce
Dash Tabasco sauce
4 tbsps chicken stock

1. Tie the legs of each hen together and tuck them under the wing tips.

2. Put the paprika, mustard, ginger, turmeric and allspice, into a small bowl and mix together well.

3. Rub the spice mixture evenly on all sides of the four birds, taking great care to push some behind the wings and into the joints.

4. Refrigerate the game hens for at least 1 hour.

5. Arrange the hens in a roasting pan. Melt the butter and brush it evenly over the birds. Roast in a preheated oven, 350°F, for 20 minutes, brushing with the roasting juices during this time.

6. Put the chili sauce, plum chutney, brown sauce, Worcestershire sauce, soy sauce and Tabasco and chicken stock into a small bowl and mix well.

7. Brush about half of this sauce over the birds. Return to the oven and cook for a further 40 minutes.

8. Brush the hens twice more with the remaining sauce mixture during this final cooking time so that the skins become brown and crisp.

Step 1 Tie the legs of each bird together with trussing thread and tuck them under the wing tips.

Step 3 Rub the poussins all over with the spice mixture, pressing it down into the wings and joints.

Cook's Notes

Time
Preparation takes about 25 minutes, plus 1 hour standing time. Cooking takes 60-70 minutes, depending on the size of the birds.

Variation
Use pigeons or grouse instead of the Cornish game hens in this recipe.

Serving Idea
Serve with fresh cooked pasta and a large salad.

Freezing
This dish freezes well for up to 3 months.

SERVES 4

SPICED PORK

*Five spice is a ready-prepared spicy powder which can easily be obtained
from delicatessens or ethnic supermarkets. It is used in this
dish with ginger and pepper to make a typical Szechwan meal.*

1lb fillet pork
5 tbsps sesame oil
One 1-inch piece fresh ginger, peeled and chopped
1¼ tsps black peppercorns
1¼ tsps five spice powder
¼ cup dry sherry
⅔ cup light stock
3 tbsps honey
4 green onions, cut into diagonal slices
⅓ cup bamboo shoots, shredded
1 large ripe mango, peeled and flesh sliced

1. Using a sharp knife, finely slice the pork fillets into thin strips.

Step 1 Using a sharp knife, shred the pork into thin strips.

2. Put the oil into a wok or large frying pan, and heat gently. Add the ginger and stir this into the oil. Fry quickly for 20-30 seconds.

Step 3 Stir-fry the meat with the oil and ginger.

Step 5 Add the onions, bamboo shoots and mango to the cooked pork, stirring continuously to cook evenly.

3. Add the sliced meat to the wok and stir-fry for 4-5 minutes, or until the meat is well cooked and tender.

4. Stir the peppercorns, five spice powder, sherry, stock and honey into the meat. Mix well and bring to the boil.

5. Add all the remaining ingredients to the wok and cook quickly, stirring all the time for a further 3 minutes.

6. Serve immediately.

Cook's Notes

Time
Preparation takes 25 minutes, cooking takes about 10 minutes.

Variation
Use chicken instead of pork in this recipe.

Serving Idea
Serve with rice or Chinese noodles.

SERVES 4

SWEET PEPPER STEAKS

*The sweet peppers in this recipe refer only to the vegetable and not
to the flavor of this dish. Peppers, mustard and capers blend
together to make a delicious spicy sauce without the need for added salt.*

4 sirloin steaks, approximately 4oz each in weight
2 cloves garlic, minced
Freshly ground black pepper
4 tbsps vegetable oil
2 shallots, finely chopped
5 tbsps capers
1 cup sliced mushrooms
2½ tbsps all-purpose flour
1¼ cups dark stock
5 tsps ready-made mustard
2½ tsps Worcestershire sauce
10 tbsps white wine
2½ tsps lemon juice
Pinch each of dried thyme and rosemary
8 baby corn on the cobs, cut in half lengthwise
1 green pepper, seeded and finely sliced
1 red pepper, seeded and finely sliced
1 yellow pepper, seeded and finely sliced
4 tomatoes, peeled, seeded and cut into thin strips

1. Lay the steaks onto a board and rub both surfaces of each with the garlic and black pepper. Refrigerate for 30 minutes.

2. Heat the oil in a large frying pan and quickly fry the steaks for 1 minute on each side. Remove the steaks from the pan and set aside.

3. Add the shallot, capers and mushrooms to the oil and meat juices in the frying pan. Cook for about 1 minute.

4. Sprinkle the flour over the vegetables and fry gently until it begins to brown. Pour over the stock and stir well, adding the mustard, Worcestershire sauce, wine, lemon juice, thyme and rosemary, as the sauce thickens.

5. Return the steaks to the sauce mixture along with the corn, peppers and tomatoes. Simmer for 6-8 minutes, or until the steaks are cooked, but still pink in the center. Serve at once.

Step 4 Sprinkle the flour over the cooked vegetables and fry gently to brown lightly.

Step 5 Stir the corn, peppers and tomatoes into the sauce, mixing well to coat evenly.

Cook's Notes

Time
Preparation takes about 30 minutes, plus 30 minutes chiling time. Cooking takes 20 minutes.

Preparation
It is important to fry the steaks initially on both sides as this helps to seal in the meats juices.

Serving Idea
Serve the steaks with rice or jacket potatoes.

SERVES 6

CHOCOLATE BRANDY MOUSSE

Chocolate and brandy blend together to create a delicious mousse which sets to a rich cream in the refrigerator.

6oz unsweetened chocolate
5½ tbsps water
1¼ tbsps unsalted butter
3 eggs, separated
2½ tbsps brandy
5 tbsps grated chocolate

1. Break the chocolate into small pieces and place in a large bowl with the water.

2. Stand the bowl over a saucepan which has been half filled with simmering water. Stir the chocolate and water together until they melt and combine thoroughly.

3. Remove the bowl from the saucepan and allow to cool slightly.

4. Cut the butter into small dice and add this to the melted chocolate, stirring it gently to blend it in as it melts.

5. Beat the egg yolks, one at a time, into the melted chocolate mixture, then stir in the brandy.

6. Put the egg whites into a large bowl and whip them with an electric or hand mixer, until they are stiff, but not dry.

7. Fold these carefully into the chocolate mixture.

8. Divide the chocolate mousse between 6 serving dishes and chill overnight before serving.

9. Sprinkle with grated chocolate to serve.

Step 2 Melt the chocolate in a large bowl placed over a pan of simmering water.

Step 7 Carefully fold the whipped egg whites into the chocolate mixture using a spatula or metal spoon.

Cook's Notes

 Time
Preparation takes 20 minutes, cooking takes about 10 minutes.

 Variation
Add half a teaspoon of grated orange rind and 2½ tbsps Cointreau in place of the brandy in this recipe.

 Watchpoint
Take great care not to melt the chocolate too quickly or it will separate.

SERVES 6

HONEY AND APPLE TART

This delicious apple flan is wonderful served either hot or cold.

¾ cup whole-wheat flour
¾ cup all-purpose white flour
6 tbsps unsalted butter
1 egg yolk
3¾ tbsps cold water
1¼ cups unsweetened apple purée
1¼ tbsps honey
2 egg yolks
2½ tbsps ground almonds
3 large eating apples, quartered, cored and thinly sliced
Little pale soft brown sugar
3¾ tbsps clear honey, warmed to glaze

Step 4 Pinch the edges of the flan up, and prick the base with a fork.

1. Put the flours into a large bowl.

2. Cut the butter into the flour until the mixture resembles fine breadcrumbs.

3. Beat the egg yolk and 2½ tbsps of the water together. Stir this into the dry ingredients, mixing to a firm soft dough and adding a little extra water if necessary.

4. Roll the dough on a lightly floured surface and line a 9-inch loose-bottom, fluted flan ring. Pinch up the edges well and prick the base to prevent it from rising during cooking.

5. Mix the apple purée with the honey, egg yolks and ground almonds, stirring well to blend thoroughly.

6. Spread this apple mixture evenly over the base of the pastry case.

7. Arrange the apple slices, overlapping slightly, in circles on the top of the apple and almond filling.

Step 7 Arrange the apple slices, overlapping each slice slightly in circles, on the top of the apple and almond filling.

8. Sprinkle the top of the flan lightly with a little soft brown sugar, and bake in a preheated oven 375°F for 35-40 minutes, or until the apples are just beginning to go golden brown.

9. As soon as the flan is removed from the oven, carefully brush the top with the warmed honey glaze.

Cook's Notes

Time
Preparation takes 45 minutes, cooking takes about 40 minutes.

Serving Idea
Serve with fresh whipped cream.

Watchpoint
If the apples begin to brown before the end of cooking time, cover the tart with aluminum foil to prevent any further coloring.

SERVES 6-8

PRUNE, APRICOT AND NUT SHORTCAKE

This sumptuous dessert has a nutty shortcake pastry for its base.

¾ cup dried apricots
¾ cup dried prunes
1¼ cups red wine, or dry cider
½ cup unsalted butter
⅓ cup soft brown sugar
1 cup all-purpose flour
⅓ cup ground hazelnuts
3¾ tbsps finely chopped walnuts
2½ tbsps clear honey, warmed

Step 4 Work the chopped walnuts into the pastry as you knead it.

Step 3 Gradually fold the ground hazelnuts and flour into the creamed butter and sugar until it forms a soft dough.

Step 5 Press the shortcake pastry evenly over the base of a loose-bottomed flan ring.

1. Put the apricots and prunes into a large bowl. Warm the wine or cider, and pour it over the dried fruit. Leave to stand for 4 hours minimum.

2. Put the butter and sugar into a large bowl and cream it together until it becomes light and fluffy.

3. Gradually stir in the flour and ground hazelnuts.

4. Knead the dough lightly until it is smooth, working in the chopped walnuts as you go.

5. Press the shortcake dough evenly over the base of a 9-inch fluted loose-bottomed flan ring. Prick the surface of the dough with a fork and bake in a preheated oven,

375°F, for 15 minutes.

6. Remove the prunes and apricots from the soaking liquid and drain them thoroughly on paper towels.

7. Remove the shortcake from the oven and arrange the fruit over the hot shortcake.

8. Cover the tart with aluminum foil and return to the oven for a further 10 minutes.

9. Remove the shortcake carefully from its pan and arrange on a serving plate.

10. While the shortcake is still hot, brush the fruit with the warmed honey to glaze.

Cook's Notes

Time
Preparation takes 30 minutes, plus soaking time. Cooking takes 25 minutes.

Watchpoint
If the shortcake mixture is too soft to handle, chill it in a refrigerator for 30 minutes.

Freezing
This dessert freezes well for up to 2 months, but should be glazed just before serving.

SERVES 4

SPICED CRÈME BRÛLÉE

Delight your guests with this unusual variation of a classic dish.

1¼ cups milk
1 stick cinnamon
2½ tbsps whole coriander seeds
1 vanilla bean
4 egg yolks
2 tbsps cornstarch
⅓ cup superfine sugar
1¼ cups heavy cream
4 tbsps demerara or light soft brown sugar

1. Put the milk into a heavy-based saucepan and add the cinnamon, coriander and vanilla bean. Heat gently until the mixture begins to boil. Remove from the heat and cool completely.

2. In a bowl, whip the egg yolks, cornstarch and the sugar together to form a soft, light mousse.

3. Strain the milk through a sieve to remove the spices. Put the strained milk into a saucepan along with the cream, and heat until just below boiling point.

4. Beat the hot milk and cream into the egg yolk mixture, pouring gradually and mixing constantly to ensure a smooth batter.

5. Rinse out the saucepan and return the custard to it. Cook over a very gentle heat until almost boiling, stirring all the time with a wooden spoon until the mixture is thick enough to coat the back of it.

6. Divide the custard equally between 4 heat resistant serving dishes. Chill until set.

7. Stand the individual custards into a roasting pan and surround them with ice. Preheat a broiler to its highest temperature.

8. Sprinkle 1 tbsps of the brown sugar evenly over the top of each custard and then put under the broiler. Turn the custards frequently and move the pan around until the sugar melts and caramelizes. Discard the ice and return the custards to the refrigerator. Chill until the sugar layer is hard and crisp.

Step 2 Whip the egg yolks, cornstarch and sugar together until they are light and creamy. When lifted, this mixture should leave a trail on its surface.

Step 5 Cook the custard very gently until it is thick enough to coat the back of a wooden spoon.

Step 7 Stand the dishes of custard in a roasting pan and surround them with broken ice to prevent the custards from heating when broiled.

Cook's Notes

Time
Preparation takes 15 minutes, cooking takes 30 minutes.

Serving Idea
Serve with cookies or fresh fruit.

 Watchpoint
Do not boil either the milk and cream mixture or the egg yolk mixture, as this will result in curdling and the custard will not be smooth.

SERVES 4

CINNAMON CŒUR À LA CRÈME WITH RASPBERRY SAUCE

Delicious cinnamon creams are complemented delightfully by the sharp raspberry sauce.

1 cup cream cheese
1½ cups whipping cream
¾ cup powdered sugar, sifted
2½ tsps ground cinnamon
½lb fresh raspberries
⅛ cup powdered sugar

1. Put the cream cheese into a large bowl along with 5 tbsps of the cream. Whip with an electric mixer until the mixture is light and fluffy.

2. Mix in the ¾ cup of powdered sugar and the cinnamon, stirring well until all ingredients are well blended.

3. Whip the remaining cream in another bowl until it forms soft peaks.

4. Fold the cream into the cheese mixture with a metal spoon.

5. Line four individual Cœur à la Crème molds with dampened cheesecloth, extending the material beyond the edges of the molds.

6. Spoon the cheese mixture into the mold and spread out evenly, pressing down well to remove any air bubbles.

7. Fold the overlapping edges of the cheesecloth over the top of the mixture, and refrigerate the molds on a rack placed over a tray, for at least 8 hours.

8. Purée the raspberries in a liquidizer or food processor, and press through a nylon sieve to remove all the seeds.

Step 5 Line four individual Cœur à la Crème molds with dampened cheesecloth, extending the material beyond the edges of the molds.

Step 7 Stand the Cœur à la Crème molds on a rack over a tray to collect the drips when refrigerated.

9. Blend the ⅛ cup of powdered sugar into the fruit purée to sweeten.

10. Carefully remove the cheesecloth from the cream cheese hearts, and place each one on a serving dish.

11. Spoon a little of the sauce over each heart and serve the remainder separately.

Cook's Notes

Time
Preparation takes 15 minutes, plus overnight refrigerating.

Preparation
It is important to use proper Cœur à la Crème moulds as these have small holes in the base which allow any excess liquid to drain off during the chilling time.

Serving Idea
Serve these cream cheese desserts with a little extra whipped cream and candied rose petals.

MAKES 10-12 COOKIES
SAFFRON COOKIES

The use of sweet spices in baking will reduce the necessity to add salt to recipes.

½ cup milk
Good pinch saffron
2 cups self-rising flour
½ cup unsalted butter
¾ cup currants
¾ tsp allspice
⅕ cup candied peel
⅓ cup superfine sugar
1 egg, beaten

1. Heat 5 tbsps of the milk in a small saucepan and add the saffron. Allow to stand for 10-15 minutes to infuse.

2. Sift the flour into a large bowl and cut the butter into this with a knife, until it is reduced to very small pieces.

3. Stir the currants, allspice, peel and sugar into the flour and butter mixture.

4. Make a well in the center of the flour and stir in the saffron milk and the remainder of the milk. Mix well to form a soft dough

5. Turn the dough onto a lightly floured board and knead until smooth.

6. Roll the dough into a circle approximately ½-inch thick. Cut into 10-12 rounds with a 3-inch biscuit cutter.

7. Arrange the individual rounds on a lightly greased cookie sheet, and brush the top with a little beaten egg.

8. Bake the cakes in a preheated oven, 350°F, for 20-30 minutes, until they are well risen and golden brown.

Step 1 Allow the saffron to infuse in the hot milk until it is golden.

Step 2 Using a round-bladed knife, cut the butter into the flour until it is finely chopped.

Step 4 Mix the milk into the flour from the center of the bowl, drawing the flour into the liquid gradually.

Cook's Notes

Time
Preparation takes 15 minutes, cooking will take 20-30 minutes.

Cook's Tip
Do not be tempted to use too much saffron; a little will go a very long way.

Freezing
These cookies freeze very well for up to 1 month.

MAKES ONE 7-inch SQUARE CAKE

GINGERBREAD

Molasses and fresh ginger combine to make this favorite family cake.

½ cup unsalted butter
½ cup molasses
1¼ cups light soft brown sugar
¼ cup hot water
2½ cups all-purpose flour
2½ tsps baking powder
2½ tsps fresh ginger, peeled and grated
1¼ tsps grated nutmeg
1 egg, beaten

Step 4 Gradually beat in the treacle, using a wooden spoon and drawing the flour from the outside into the center.

Step 1 Melt the butter, molasses and sugar together in a large saucepan.

Step 6 The cake is done when a skewer inserted into the center comes out clean.

1. Put the butter into a large saucepan, along with the molasses and sugar. Heat gently, stirring all the time, until the sugar and butter have melted together.

2. Pour in the hot water, mix well and set aside.

3. Sift the flour with the baking powder into a large bowl. Make a well in the center, and add the ginger, nutmeg and beaten egg.

4. Gradually beat in the molasses, using a wooden spoon and drawing the flour from the outside into the center

gradually.

5. Line the base of the cake pan with silicone or lightly greased wax paper.

6. Pour the gingerbread mixture into the cake pan, and bake in a preheated oven 325°F, for 1-1½ hours, testing during this time with a skewer; which should come out clean when the cake is cooked.

7. Allow the cake to cool in the pan, before turning out onto a wire rack.

Cook's Notes

Time
Preparation takes about 15 minutes, cooking takes 1-1½ hours.

Variation
Add 2oz chopped mixed fruit to the gingerbread mixture along with the spices.

Serving Idea
Serve as a dessert with a lemon sauce.

Freezing
This cake freezes well for up to 1 month.

MAKES ONE 8-inch ROUND CAKE

ALMOND LAYER CAKE

*Definitely not for the diet conscious, but delicious for those wishing
to sin. This wonderful creamy gateau is ideal
for serving with tea, or even as a dessert.*

½ cup dried white breadcrumbs
⅓ cup milk
1¼ tbsps rum
6 tbsps unsalted butter or margarine
½ cup superfine sugar
6 eggs, separated
½ cup ground roasted almonds
2½ cups heavy cream
2½ tbsps powdered sugar
2oz roasted almonds, finely chopped
Whole blanched almonds, lightly toasted for decoration

1. Put the breadcrumbs into a large bowl and pour over the milk and 1 tbsp of the rum. Allow to stand for 15 minutes or until the liquid has been completely absorbed.

2. Put the butter in a large bowl and beat until soft. Gradually add the sugar and continue mixing until it is light and fluffy.

3. Beat the egg yolks, one at a time, into the butter mixture. Stir well to prevent it curdling.

4. Add the soaked breadcrumbs to the egg and butter mixture, folding them well to blend evenly.

5. Whip the egg whites until they are stiff, but not dry. Fold these into the egg and butter mixture, along with the ground almonds.

6. Lightly grease three 8-inch round cake pans, and dust each one lightly with a little flour. Line the base of each pan with silicone paper or lightly greased wax paper.

7. Divide the cake mixture equally between the three pans. Bake in a preheated oven 350°F, for 30-35 minutes, until well risen and golden brown.

8. Allow the cakes to cool briefly in the pans before gently loosening the sides and turning onto a wire rack to cool completely.

9. Whip the cream until it is stiff, then beat in the powdered sugar and remaining rum.

10. Reserve one third of the cream in a separate bowl, and fold the finely chopped almonds into the remaining two-thirds.

11. Sandwich the cake layers together with the almond cream, then spread the plain cream onto the top, reserving some for piping.

12. Fit a pastry bag with a small fluted tip and pipe rosettes of cream onto the top of the cake. Decorate with the toasted whole almonds and serve.

Step 3 Beat the egg yolks, one at a time, into the butter and sugar mixture, mixing well to prevent curdling.

Step 11 Sandwich the layers of the cake together with the almond cream, pressing them down gently so that the cream shows around the edge.

Cook's Notes

Time
Preparation takes 40 minutes, cooking takes 35 minutes.

Cook's Tip
Refrigerate the cream for at least 2 hours before whipping, to obtain better results.

Freezing
The almond cakes can be frozen for up to 1 month, but should be filled and decorated just before serving or they will become too soggy.

VITAMIN
RICH

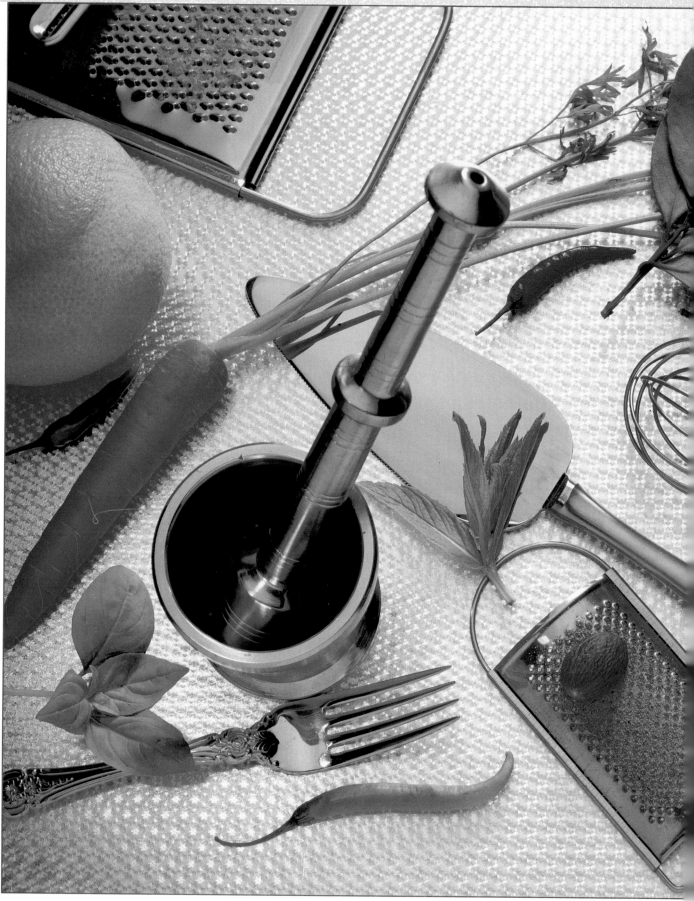

VITAMIN RICH

Introduction

Vitamins are substances that are vital to the maintenance of our bodies, yet so much is written concerning these invisible, potent elements in our food that few of us can tell fact from fiction.

There are many different vitamins, but we only need each in very small quantities, and if we maintain a well balanced and varied diet, the food we eat will generally provide us with more than enough vitamins for our daily needs. In certain circumstances, however, such as during pregnancy, illness or in old age, vitamin supplements may be required, and in these cases professional advice should be sought.

Vitamins are mainly identified by letter, but this in no way indicates their order of importance. In the case of vitamin B, there are several complex variations of vitamins within the one heading, and this is called the "B complex". The table below gives general guidance on some of the main vitamins, their source and function.

VITAMIN	SOURCE	FUNCTION
A	Oily fish, fats, offal, carrots, green vegetables, tomatoes, watercress	General growth, good eyesight, healthy skin
B.1	Yeast extract, wheatgerm, peanuts, whole-wheat bread, eggs, pulses	Assists the nervous system and metabolism. Is water soluble and therefore easily lost in cooking
B.2	Milk, dairy products, almonds, mushrooms, pulses, red meat, green vegetables	Assists the metabolism and maintains health of mouth, lips and skin
B.3	Milk, eggs, yeast extract, red meat, dried apricots	Essential to the nervous system
B.6	Yeast, whole cereal products, offal, dairy products, bananas, leaf vegetables	Helps production of new cells and promotes nervous health
B.12	Offal, meat, eggs, cheese, milk	Assists the production of red blood cells
C	Fruit and vegetables	Helps the body resist infection, promotes good skin, helps absorption of iron
D	Oily fish, fats, dairy products, offal, red meat	Helps promote strong bones and teeth. Is produced in the body when there is exposure to sunlight
E	Whole cereal products, eggs, nuts, vegetable oil and whole-wheat flour	Necessary for upkeep of blood cells, tissues and membranes
K	Widely available in many foods such as green vegetables, eggs and cereals	Helps blood to clot and assists in the healing of wounds

SERVES 6-8

COUNTRYSIDE TERRINE

This impressive terrine looks very professional yet is simple to make.

1lb pigs' liver, ground
¾lb lean pork, ground
½lb pork sausagemeat
1 clove garlic, minced
2 shallots, finely chopped
3¾ tbsps Cognac
¾ tsp ground allspice
Salt and freshly ground black pepper
1¼ tsps chopped fresh thyme or sage
½lb bacon, rind and any bones removed
2½ tbsps heavy cream
¼lb smoked tongue or ham, cut into ¼-inch cubes
1 large bay leaf

1. Preheat oven to 350°F.

2. In a large bowl, mix together the ground liver and pork, sausagemeat, garlic, shallots, Cognac, allspice, salt, pepper, and thyme. Stir with a wooden spoon until the ingredients are evenly mixed, but still coarse in texture.

3. Lay the strips of bacon on a flat surface and stretch them with the back of a knife.

4. Line a 2lb loaf pan evenly with the strips of bacon, overlapping each strip slightly to avoid any of the terrine mixture pushing through during cooking.

5. Add the cream, cubed tongue and ham to the liver and pork mixture, blending with your hands to keep the texture coarse.

6. Press the terrine mixture into the bacon-lined loaf pan, spreading it evenly, and pushing down lightly to remove any air bubbles.

7. Place the bay leaf on the top and fold over any overlapping edges of bacon.

8. Cover the dish with a tight-fitting lid or two layers of aluminum foil.

9. Stand the loaf pan in a roasting pan and pour enough water around it to come halfway up the sides of the dish.

10. Bake the terrine for 2 hours, or until the juices run clear when a knife is inserted into the center.

11. Remove the lid or foil and replace this with some fresh foil.

12. Weigh down the terrine with cans of food or balance scale weights. Allow the terrine to cool at room temperature, then refrigerate it overnight if possible, still weighted, until it is completely chilled and firm.

13. To serve, remove the weights and foil and carefully turn the terrine out onto a serving plate. Scrape away any fat or jelly that may be on the outside of the terrine, and cut into slices just before serving.

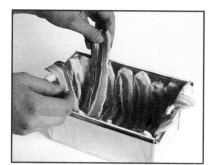

Step 4 Line a 2lb loaf pan evenly with the strips of bacon, overlapping each strip slightly.

Step 12 Cover the terrine with a double thickness of fresh foil and weight it down with cans or scale weights.

Cook's Notes

 Time
Preparation takes about 25 minutes, plus refrigeration time. Cooking takes approximately 2 hours.

 **Freezing**
This recipe will freeze well for up to 3 months. It should be packed in plastic wrap and not aluminum or metal foil.

 Vitamin Content
This recipe is an extremely good source of all the B complex vitamins.

SERVES 4

TARAMASALATA

This well known, classic Greek appetizer is a delicious way of improving your intake of vitamins B and C.

¼ cup smoked cod roe
6 slices white bread, crusts removed
1 lemon
1 small onion, finely chopped
7½ tbsps olive oil
Black olives and chopped fresh parsley, for garnish

1. Cut the cod roe in half and scrape out the center into a bowl. Discard the skin.

Step 1 Cut the cods roe in half and carefully remove the soft insides using a small spoon. Discard the skin.

Step 2 Squeeze the soaked bread to remove the excess moisture.

Step 5 Gradually add the oil to the fish mixture, beating continuously and very vigorously between additions to prevent curdling.

2. Put the bread into a bowl along with ⅔ cup warm water. Allow the bread to soak for about 10 minutes, then drain off the water and squeeze the bread until it is almost dry. Add the bread to the bowl containing the cod roe.

3. Squeeze the lemon and add the juice to the bread and roe, stirring it well.

4. Put the cod roe mixture into a blender or food processor, along with the onion. Process until the ingredients form a smooth paste.

5. Return the blended cod roe mixture to a bowl and gradually beat in the oil, a little at a time, as if making mayonnaise. Beat the mixture very thoroughly between additions with an eggbeater or wooden spoon.

6. Refrigerate the taramasalata for at least ½ hour to chill thoroughly.

7. Transfer the mixture to a serving bowl and garnish with the black olives and chopped parsley.

Cook's Notes

Time
Preparation takes about 15-25 minutes, plus refrigeration time.

Cook's Tip
Prepare the taramasalata in advance, but remove it from the refrigerator 20 minutes before serving.

Serving Idea
Warm pitta breads and toasts, cut into fingers and used for dipping, make an excellent accompaniment.

Watchpoint
Do not add the oil too quickly or the mixture will curdle. If it does, add a little more soaked bread to draw it back together again.

Vitamin Content
Vitamin B complex and also vitamin C.

SERVES 4

WATERCRESS SOUP

Watercress is packed with vitamins A, C and K, and makes delicious soup.

¼ cup butter
1 leek, cleaned and thinly sliced
½lb potatoes, peeled and sliced thinly
2½ cups chicken stock
Pinch grated nutmeg
Salt and freshly ground black pepper
4 good bunches of watercress, washed and trimmed
3¾ tbsps cream
Few extra sprigs of watercress for garnish

1. Melt the butter in a large saucepan and gently cook the leek until it is just soft, stirring frequently to prevent it from browning.

2. Add the potatoes, stock, nutmeg and seasoning to the saucepan. Bring to the boil, then cover and simmer for 15 minutes.

3. Add the watercress and simmer for a further 10 minutes.

4. Cool the soup slightly, then using a food processor or blender, process until the vegetables are very finely chopped. Rinse the saucepan and stand a fine meshed sieve over the cleaned pan.

5. Push the puréed soup through the sieve using the back of a wooden spoon, working the watercress and vegetables through the mesh until only the tough stalks remain and the soup in the pan is a fine purée.

6. Adjust the seasoning and stir the cream into the soup. Reheat gently, taking care not to boil it. Serve garnished with the reserved watercress sprigs and a little cream if desired.

Step 1 Slowly soften the leek in the melted butter, stirring to prevent it from browning.

Step 4 Blend the soup in a food processor or liquidizer until the vegetables are very finely chopped.

Step 5 Push the soup through a fine meshed sieve using a wooden spoon, work the vegetable pulp through until only the tough stalks remain in the sieve.

Cook's Notes

Time
Preparation takes 15 minutes, cooking takes about 45 minutes.

Serving Idea
Chill the soup, and serve on a bed of crushed ice for a delicious variation.

Vitamin Content
Watercress is an excellent source of vitamins A, C and K.

SERVES 4

GAZPACHO

*Gazpacho is a typically Spanish soup which is served well chilled,
accompanied by a selection of fresh vegetables.*

1lb ripe tomatoes
1 onion, peeled and chopped
1 green pepper, seeded and diced
½ cucumber, chopped
2½ tbsps stale white breadcrumbs
2 cloves garlic, minced
2½ tbsps red wine vinegar
2½ cups tomato juice
Salt and freshly ground black pepper

Accompaniments
½ cucumber, diced
10 green onions, chopped
½lb tomatoes, skinned, seeded and chopped
1 large green pepper, seeded and diced

1. Cut a small cross in the top of each of the ripe tomatoes, and plunge into a bowl of boiling water for a few seconds.

2. Carefully peel the skin away from the blanched tomatoes. Discard the skin and roughly chop the tomatoes, removing the tough stalk as you do.

3. Put the roughly chopped tomatoes into a liquidizer or food processor, along with the onion, pepper and cucumber. Blend until finely chopped.

4. Put the chopped vegetables into a bowl with the breadcrumbs, garlic, vinegar and tomato juice. Mix well to blend evenly and allow to stand for 15 minutes.

5. Season the tomato soup thoroughly, then push through a fine meshed sieve using the back of a wooden spoon and working well to press all the vegetables through, but keeping the pips out of the resulting purée.

6. Chill the soup well before serving, surrounded by bowls containing the accompaniments.

Step 2 Carefully peel the skin away from the blanched tomatoes using a sharp knife.

Step 5 Push the puréed vegetables through a nylon sieve using the back of a wooden spoon, working until all the pulp has been pressed through and the tomato pips remain.

Cook's Notes

Time
Preparation takes approximately 20 minutes, plus chiling time.

Serving Idea
Serve the individual bowls of soup on crushed ice.

Freezing
This soup is ideal for freezing.

V **Vitamin Content**
Extremely high in vitamin C and the tomatoes are a good source of vitamin A.

SERVES 4

MUSSEL SOUP

Shellfish contain a multitude of vitamins and minerals, especially vitamins A, E, D and K, and this soup is, therefore, a delicious way of making sure you have a good supply of all of these.

2 quarts fresh mussels
¼ cup butter
2 onions, peeled and finely chopped
2 cloves garlic, minced
1¼ cups dry white wine
1¼ cups water
2½ tbsps lemon juice
1 cup fresh white breadcrumbs
2½ tbsps freshly chopped parsley
Salt and freshly ground black pepper

1. Scrub the mussels with a stiff brush and remove any barnacle shells or pieces of seaweed that are attached to them.

2. Tap each mussel sharply to make sure that it closes tightly.

3. Melt the butter in a large saucepan and gently fry the onions and garlic until they are soft, but not browned.

4. Add the mussels, wine, water and lemon juice to the pan, and bring to the boil. Season with salt and pepper, then cover and cook for approximately 10 minutes or until all the mussel shells have completely opened.

5. Discard any mussels which have not opened fully.

6. Strain the mussels through a colander and return the juices and stock to the saucepan. Put the mussels in a serving tureen and keep warm.

7. Add the breadcrumbs and the parsley to the mussel juices and bring them to the boil. Adjust the seasoning, and serve over the mussels in the tureen. Serve immediately.

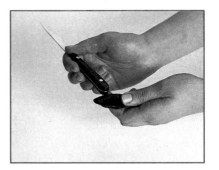

Step 2 Tap each mussel sharply with the handle of a knife to make sure that they shut tightly. Discard any that do not.

Step 1 Scrub the mussels with a stiff brush, removing any barnacles and pieces of seaweed which may be attached to the shells.

Step 4 Cook the mussels until they have all completely opened. Discard any that remain closed.

Cook's Notes

Time
Preparation takes 15 minutes, cooking takes approximately 20 minutes.

Watchpoint
When cooking fresh mussels, great care must be taken to ensure that they are safe to eat. Discard any that do not shut tightly before cooking, or do not open after cooking.

Serving Idea
Serve with warm French bread.

Vitamin Content
This soup contains vitamins A, B, E and K.

SERVES 4-6

SPINACH GNOCCHI

Gnocchi are delicious spinach and cheese dumplings which can be served as a healthy appetizer or snack.

¼lb chopped, frozen spinach
½lb ricotta cheese, crumbled
6 tbsps Parmesan cheese, finely grated
Salt and freshly ground pepper
Pinch freshly grated nutmeg
1 egg, lightly beaten
3½ tbsps butter

1. Defrost the spinach and press it between two plates to extract all the moisture.

Step 1 Press the spinach between two plates to remove excess moisture

2. Mix the spinach with the ricotta cheese, half the Parmesan cheese, the salt, pepper and nutmeg. Gradually add the egg, beating well until the mixture holds together when shaped.

3. With floured hands, shape the mixture into oval shapes. Use about 1 tbsp mixture for each gnocchi.

4. Lower into simmering water 3 or 4 at a time and allow to cook gently until the gnocchi float to the surface (about 1-2 minutes).

5. Remove with a draining spoon and place in a well buttered ovenproof dish.

6. When all the gnocchi are cooked, sprinkle on the re-

Step 3 Shape the gnocchi mixture with well-floured hands into ovals or balls.

Step 4 The gnocchi will float to the surface of the water when cooked. Remove with a draining spoon.

maining Parmesan cheese and dot with the remaining butter.

7. Reheat for 10 minutes in a hot oven and brown under a preheated broiler before serving.

Cook's Notes

Time
Preparation takes 15 minutes, cooking takes about 20 minutes.

Variation
Accompany with a tomato or cheese sauce and a salad for a light meal.

Vitamin Content
Spinach is a good source of vitamin A and the cheese provides vitamin B.

SERVES 4

ZUCCHINI SALAD

Raw vegetables are full of vitamins, and zucchini in particular has a delicious taste and texture.

½lb macaroni
4 tomatoes
4-5 zucchini, sliced thinly
8 stuffed green olives, sliced
7½ tbsps French dressing

1. Put the macaroni into a large saucepan and cover with boiling water. Add a little salt and simmer for 10 minutes, or until tender but still firm. Rinse in cold water and drain well.

2. Cut a small cross in the tops of each tomato and plunge into boiling water for 30 seconds.

3. Carefully remove the skins from the blanched tomatoes, using a sharp knife. Chop the tomatoes coarsely.

4. Mix all the ingredients in a large bowl and chill in the refrigerator for 30 minutes before serving.

Step 1 Rinse the macaroni in lots of cold water, then drain well forking it occasionally to prevent it sticking together.

Step 4 Mix all the ingredients together well, stirring thoroughly to blend the dressing in evenly.

Cook's Notes

Time
Preparation takes 15 minutes, cooking takes approximately 10 minutes.

Variation
Use any other pasta shape of your choice.

Preparation
If you prefer, the zucchini can be blanched in boiling water for 1 minute, then drained and cooled before mixing with the salad ingredients.

V Vitamin Content
This recipe is high in vitamin C from the zucchini and tomatoes, vitamin A from the tomatoes and vitamin B from the pasta.

SERVES 4-6

WATERCRESS AND ORANGE SALAD

This colorful salad combination is ideal served with cold meats or fish.

3 large bunches of watercress
4 oranges
7½ tbsps vegetable oil
Juice and rind of 1 orange
Pinch sugar
1¼ tsps lemon juice
Salt and freshly ground black pepper

1. Wash the watercress and carefully cut away any thick stalks. Break the watercress into small sprigs, discarding any yellow leaves.

2. Carefully remove the peel and pith from the oranges using a sharp knife. Catch any juice that spills in a small bowl.

3. Cutting carefully, remove the fleshy segments from between the thin membrane inside the orange. Squeeze any juice from the orange membrane into the bowl with the juice from the peel.

4. Arrange the watercress with the orange segments on a serving dish.

5. Put the remaining ingredients into the bowl with the reserved orange juice, and mix together well.

6. Pour the salad dressing over the oranges and watercress just before serving, to prevent the watercress from going limp.

Step 1 Break the watercress into small sprigs, discarding any yellow leaves.

Step 2 Carefully peel the oranges using a sharp knife, and collecting any juices in a small bowl.

Step 3 Cut the orange segments carefully from between the inner membranes using a sharp knife.

Cook's Notes

Time
Preparation takes approximately 20 minutes.

Serving Idea
Serve this salad on a bed of finely grated carrot.

Variation
Use grapefruit instead of the oranges, and chicory instead of the watercress.

V Vitamin Content
This salad is extremely high in vitamin C, and if served with carrot is also a good source of vitamin A.

CHEESE SALAD

This cheese salad is distinctly Greek in origin, and is ideal as an appetizer as well as being substantial enough to serve as a light lunch.

½ small head of endive or Crisp lettuce
½ small Iceberg lettuce
1 small cucumber
4 large tomatoes
8-10 pitted green or black olives, halved
1 medium-sized Spanish or red onion, peeled and sliced
¼lb feta cheese
6 tbsps olive oil
2½ tbsps red wine vinegar
1¼ tsps chopped fresh oregano
¾ tsp freshly ground sea salt
½ tsp freshly ground black pepper
¾ tsp ready made German mustard

1. Wash the endive and lettuce leaves thoroughly. Pat them dry with paper towels and tear into bite-sized pieces.

2. Thinly slice the cucumber, peeling it if you wish.

3. Cut a small cross into the top of each tomato and plunge into boiling water for 30 seconds.

4. Carefully peel the skins from the blanched tomatoes and slice the flesh crosswise.

5. Put the endive, lettuce, cucumber, tomatoes, olives and onion into a serving bowl and toss them together until well mixed.

6. Cut the feta cheese into ½-inch cubes. Sprinkle these

Step 1 Tear the lettuce and endive into pieces to prevent excessive bruising and destruction of vitamins in the leaves.

Step 4 Using a sharp knife, slice the peeled tomatoes crosswise.

cubes over the salad in the serving bowl.

7. Put all the remaining ingredients into a small bowl and whisk together using a fork or small eggbeater.

8. Pour the dressing over the salad and serve immediately.

Cook's Notes

Time
Preparation takes 10-12 minutes.

Serving Idea
Serve with jacket potatoes or crusty French bread.

Variation
Use Cheddar or Cheshire cheese in place of the feta cheese.

Vitamin Content
Leaf vegetables such as lettuce are an excellent source of vitamin K. The tomatoes and cucumber are high in vitamin C and the cheese is a good source of vitamins B and D.

SERVES 6

ROGNONS À LA DIJONNAISE

This delicious French dish makes good use of vitamin-rich kidneys, an offal which is often underused in cookery.

½lbs lambs' kidneys
¼ cup unsalted butter
1-2 shallots, finely chopped
1¼ cups dry white wine
6 tbsps lightly salted butter, softened
3½ tbsps·Dijon mustard
Salt, black pepper and lemon juice, to taste
2½ tbsps chopped parsley

Step 2 Trim away any hard core from the center of each kidney half using a small pair of sharp scissors.

Step 1 Trim the fat from each kidney and cut them in half lengthwise.

Step 8 Whisk the butter, mustard, salt, pepper and lemon juice into the reduced sauce using a fork or eggbeater and beating until it is thick.

1. Trim away any fat from the kidneys and slice them in half lengthwise.

2. Carefully snip out any hard core from the center using a pair of sharp scissors.

3. Melt the unsalted butter in a large frying pan and gently sauté the kidneys, uncovered, until they are light brown on all sides.

4. Remove the kidneys from the frying pan and keep them warm.

5. Add the shallots to the meat juices in the pan and cook

for about 1 minute, stirring frequently until they are just soft.

6. Add the wine and bring to the boil, stirring constantly and scraping the pan to remove any browned juices.

7. Boil this sauce rapidly for 3-4 minutes to reduce by about half. Remove the pan from the heat.

8. Put the softened butter into the pan with the mustard and seasonings. Whisk the mixture into the reduced sauce with an eggbeater or fork.

9. Return the pan to the heat and add the kidneys and the parsley. Heat very gently for 1-2 minutes, taking care not to boil the mixture any further. Serve immediately.

Cook's Notes

Time
Preparation takes approximately 25 minutes, cooking takes 15-17 minutes.

Watchpoint
Do not overcook the kidneys or they will become tough.

Vitamin Content
Kidneys are an excellent source of vitamins A, B and D.

SERVES 6

PORK PROVENÇALE

This hearty casserole of lean pork topped with potatoes is suitable for serving as a family meal, or as part of a dinner party menu.

2lbs pork fillets
¼ cup butter
¾lb onions, peeled and thinly sliced
15oz can tomatoes
Salt and freshly ground black pepper
½ tsp dried mixed herbs
1½lbs potatoes, peeled and thinly sliced
1 tbsp chopped parsley for garnish

1. Trim the pork of any surplus fat and slice into thin strips.

2. Melt half of the butter in a large sauté pan and gently fry

Step 1 Slice the pork into thin strips using a sharp knife.

Step 4 Gently fry the onions in the meat juices until they are just soft.

the slices of meat, stirring continuously to prevent them from burning.

3. Transfer the meat to a plate and set aside.

4. Stir the onions into the meat juices in the sauté pan and cook gently until just soft.

5. Add the tomatoes to the pan along with the salt, pepper and mixed herbs. Bring to the boil, then simmer gently for about 5 minutes, or until the sauce has reduced by about a third.

6. Arrange the meat, sauce and potatoes in layers in an ovenproof serving dish, finishing with a layer of potato.

7. Melt the remaining butter and brush the top layer of potato with this.

8. Cover the dish with a lid or foil, and cook in the oven for 1½ hours at 350°F.

9. Remove the lid from the dish and continue cooking for a further 30 minutes to brown the potatoes. Sprinkle with chopped parsley before serving.

Step 6 Arrange the meat, tomato sauce and potatoes in layers in an ovenproof serving dish.

Cook's Notes

Time
Preparation takes 25 minutes, cooking takes approximately 2 hours.

Freezing
This dish will freeze very well for up to 3 months. Freeze it before the final 30 minutes cooking time, then reheat by thawing and cooking uncovered for 1 hour at 350°F.

V **Vitamin Content**
The vegetables are a good source of vitamin C, and the tomatoes also contain vitamin A.

SERVES 4

LENTIL KEDGEREE

This delicious recipe combines spiced rice with lentils and onion to make a substantial vegetarian lunch or supper dish.

1¼ cups basmati rice
1¼ cups red lentils
3¼ cups warm water
½ cup butter, or olive oil
1 medium-sized onion, peeled and chopped
¾ tsp crushed fresh root ginger
¾ tsp minced garlic
1-inch piece cinnamon stick
6 cloves
1 bay leaf
1¼ tsps ground coriander
½ tsp ground turmeric
¾ tsp freshly ground sea salt
2 green chilies, sliced in half lengthwise

1. Wash the rice and the lentils thoroughly in cold water. Drain well.

2. Put the drained rice and lentils into a large bowl and cover with the warm water. Soak for 30 minutes, then drain very thoroughly, reserving the water.

3. Heat the butter or olive oil in a large saucepan. Stir in the onion and fry gently for 2-3 minutes, stirring to prevent it burning.

4. Add the ginger, garlic, cinnamon stick, cloves and bay leaf to the onion and continue frying for 1 minute.

5. Add the rice and lentils to the fried onion, along with the coriander, turmeric, salt and green chili. Stir over the heat for 2-3 minutes, until the rice and lentils are evenly coated

Step 5 Stir-fry the rice and lentils together, making sure that they are evenly coated with the fat.

Step 6 Cook the rice and lentils until all the liquid has been absorbed, then fluff up with a fork before serving.

with fat.

6. Pour the reserved water into the rice mixture and bring to the boil. Reduce the heat and cover the pan with a tight fitting lid. Simmer for 8-10 minutes without stirring, or until the water has been completely absorbed.

7. Stir the rice and lentils together, remove and discard the chilies, and serve immediately.

Cook's Notes

Time
Preparation takes 15 minutes, plus soaking time. Cooking takes approximately 30 minutes.

Watchpoint
Great care must be taken when using fresh chilies. If any of the juice gets into your mouth or eyes, rinse with lots of cold water.

V **Vitamin Content**
Lentils and rice are both excellent sources of vitamin B.

SERVES 4

LENTIL AND VEGETABLE CURRY

Lentils are a staple ingredient in Indian cookery. This delicious vegetable curry should be made using fresh spices for the best flavor.

1¼ cups whole green lentils
2½ tbsps vegetable oil
1¼ tsps salt
¾ tsp mustard seed, crushed
1 tsp ground coriander
¾ tsp ground cumin
2 dried red chilies, crushed
1 carrot, peeled and sliced diagonally
1 potato, peeled and cubed
6-8 okra, topped and tailed, then cut into 1-inch pieces
1 small zucchini, sliced diagonally
1 small eggplant, halved and sliced
1¾ cups water
6 curry leaves
1 green chili, slit in half and chopped
1¼ tsps fresh chopped mint
1¼ tbsps fresh chopped coriander
Coriander leaves for garnish

1. Wash the lentils in warm water until it runs clear. Drain well.

2. Put the lentils into a large saucepan and pour over 2½ cups water. Simmer gently for 15-20 minutes.

3. When the lentils are soft, beat with a potato masher or eggbeater until they are puréed.

4. In a large saucepan heat the oil and gently fry the mustard seed, ground coriander, cumin and dried chilies for 1 minute.

5. Add the vegetables to the spices and cook for 2 minutes, stirring all the time, to coat them evenly in the oil and spice mixture.

6. Add the water and the puréed lentils to the vegetable mixture and stir well.

7. Add the curry leaves, chopped chili, mint and fresh coriander, then cook for 15 minutes. Serve hot, garnished with coriander leaves.

Step 3 Using a potato masher or eggbeater, break up the cooked lentils until they are well puréed.

Step 6 Stir the puréed lentils into the vegetable mixture.

Cook's Notes

Time
Preparation takes about 10 minutes, cooking takes 20-30 minutes.

Variation
Use any combination of fresh vegetables to vary this curry.

Serving Idea
Serve with boiled basmati rice.

V **Vitamin Content**
Lentils provide an excellent source of vitamin B and fresh vegetables provide vitamins A and C.

SERVES 4

BEEF WITH PINEAPPLE AND PEPPERS

This delicious sweet and sour main course is distinctly Chinese in origin.

1lb fillet or rump steak
1 small pineapple
1 green pepper
1 red pepper
1¼ tbsps peanut oil
1 onion, peeled and roughly chopped
2 cloves garlic, minced
1-inch fresh root ginger, peeled and thinly sliced
1¼ tsps sesame oil
2½ tbsps light soy sauce
1¼ tbsps dark soy sauce
1¼ tsps sugar
1¼ tbsps brown sauce
5 tbsps water
Salt and freshly ground black pepper

1. Using a sharp knife, cut the steak into thin strips.

2. Carefully peel the pineapple and cut out any eyes using a sharp knife or potato peeler. Cut the pineapple into slices and chop them into bite-sized pieces, removing the hard core.

3. Slice the green and red peppers in half. Remove and discard the cores and seeds. Chop the pepper flesh into thin strips.

4. Heat the peanut oil in a wok or large frying pan, and gently fry the onion, garlic and ginger, stirring continuously until the onion has softened slightly.

5. Add the strips of beef and the strips of pepper, and continue stir-frying for 3 minutes.

6. Add the pineapple and stir-fry again for 2 minutes.

7. Remove the meat, vegetables and fruit from the wok, and put on a plate. Set aside.

8. Stir the sesame oil into the juices in the wok and add the soy sauces, sugar, brown sauce and water. Simmer rapidly for 30 seconds to reduce and thicken.

9. Stir the fruit, vegetables and beef back into the sauce. Season, heat through and serve immediately.

Step 1 Using a sharp knife, cut the steak into thin strips.

Step 5 Stir-fry the beef and peppers with the onions in the wok.

Cook's Notes

Time
Preparation takes 30 minutes, cooking takes about 10 minutes.

Serving Idea
Serve with spring rolls and plain boiled rice.

Watchpoint
Take care not to overcook the meat and vegetables, as this will greatly reduce the vitamin content of this dish.

Vitamin Content
Steak is an excellent source of vitamin B and the vegetables and fruit are high in vitamin C.

SERVES 4
KIDNEYS WITH BACON

Stir-frying is an excellent way of cooking kidneys, as the speedy cooking ensures that they do not become tough.

1lb lambs' kidneys
2½ tbsps vegetable oil
8 strips lean bacon, cut into 1-inch strips
1 onion, peeled and chopped
3 cloves garlic, minced
1¼ tbsps tomato chutney
1¼ tbsps light soy sauce
2½ tbsps water
Salt and freshly ground black pepper
1¼ tbsps cornstarch
3¾ tbsps sherry
2 tbsps fresh chopped parsley

1. Trim the fat from the kidneys and cut each kidney in half with a sharp knife.

2. Carefully trim out the hard core from the center of each kidney with a sharp knife or scissors.

3. Cut a lattice design on the back of each kidney using a sharp knife and taking care not to cut right through.

4. Put the kidneys into a bowl and stir in the sherry. Set aside for 15 minutes to marinate.

5. Heat the oil in a large wok and fry the bacon, onion and garlic for 5 minutes, stirring continuously to prevent burning. Remove from the wok and set aside on a plate.

6. Drain the kidneys and reserve the sherry marinade. Add the kidneys to the wok and stir for 3 minutes only.

7. Stir the tomato chutney, soy sauce and water into the wok with the kidneys, then add the bacon and onion mixture. Season with salt and pepper and stir-fry gently for 5 minutes.

8. Blend the cornstarch with the sherry marinade.

9. Add 1 tbsp parsley to the cornstarch mixture and stir

Step 2 Remove the hard core from each kidney half using a sharp knife or a small pair of scissors.

Step 3 Cut a lattice design on the backs of each kidney, using a sharp knife, and taking care not to cut right through.

Step 6 Stir-fry the kidneys until they are completely browned.

this into the kidneys in the wok, mixing well until the sauce is thickened and smooth. Serve at once, sprinkled with a little extra parsley.

Cook's Notes

Time
Preparation takes 20 minutes, cooking takes 25 minutes.

Serving Idea
Serve with rice or creamed potatoes.

Vitamin Content
All offal is an excellent source of vitamins A, B and D.

SERVES 4

MONKFISH AND PEPPER KEBABS

Monkfish is ideal for making kebabs as it can be cut into firm cubes, which do not disintegrate during cooking.

8 strips of lean bacon, rind removed
1lb monkfish, skinned and cut into 1-inch pieces
1 small green pepper, seeded and cut into 1-inch pieces
1 small red pepper, seeded and cut into 1-inch pieces
12 small mushroom caps
8 bay leaves
3¾ tbsps vegetable oil
½ cup dry white wine
5 tbsps tarragon vinegar
2 shallots, finely chopped
1¼ tbsps chopped fresh tarragon
1¼ tbsps chopped fresh chervil or parsley
1 cup butter, softened
Salt and freshly ground black pepper

Step 2 Wrap each piece of fish in one of the strips of bacon.

Step 8 Add the butter gradually into the simmering wine, whisking briskly to thicken the sauce.

1. Cut the bacon strips in half lengthwise and then again in half crosswise.

2. Put a piece of the fish onto each piece of bacon and roll the bacon around the piece of fish.

3. Thread the bacon and fish rolls onto large skewers, alternating them with slices of pepper, mushroom and the bay leaves.

4. Brush the kebabs with oil and arrange on a broiler pan.

5. Preheat the broiler to hot and cook the kebabs for 10-15 minutes, turning them frequently to prevent the kebabs from burning.

6. Heat the white wine, vinegar and shallots in a small saucepan until boiling. Cook rapidly to reduce by half.

7. Add the herbs and lower the heat.

8. Using a fork or eggbeater beat the butter bit by bit into the hot wine mixture, whisking rapidly until the sauce becomes thick. Season to taste.

9. Arrange the kebabs on a serving plate and serve with a little of the sauce spooned over and the remainder in a separate jug.

Cook's Notes

Time
Preparation takes 30 minutes, cooking will take about 25 minutes.

Preparation
When making the sauce it is important to whisk briskly, or it will not thicken sufficiently.

Vitamin Content
Fish is an excellent source of vitamins A and D. Bacon is a good source of vitamin B, and peppers are high in vitamin C.

SERVES 4

SWORDFISH STEAKS WITH GREEN PEPPERCORNS AND GARLIC SAUCE

Swordfish steaks are delicious and are easily available at most good fishmongers.

2½ tbsps fresh green peppercorns
7½ tbsps lemon juice
5 tbsps olive oil
Freshly ground sea salt
4 swordfish steaks
1 egg
1 clove garlic, roughly chopped
⅔ cup oil
2½ tsps fresh oregano
Salt and freshly ground black pepper

1. Crush the green peppercorns lightly using a pestle and mortar.

2. Mix the lemon juice, olive oil and salt into the lightly crushed green peppercorns.

3. Place the swordfish steaks in a shallow ovenproof dish and pour the lemon and oil mixture over each steak. Re-frigerate overnight, turning occasionally until the fish becomes opaque.

4. Using a blender or food processor, mix together the eggs and garlic.

5. With the machine still running, gradually pour the oil through the funnel in a thin steady stream onto the egg and garlic mixture. Continue to blend until the sauce is thick.

6. Remove the leaves from the oregano sprigs and chop them finely.

7. Preheat the broiler to hot and arrange the swordfish on the broiler pan.

8. Sprinkle the chopped oregano over the swordfish steaks and season well. Cook for 15 minutes, turning them frequently and basting with the lemon and pepper marinade.

9. When the steaks are cooked, place on a serving dish and spoon the garlic mayonnaise over.

Step 1 Lightly crush the green pepper-corns using a pestle and mortar.

Step 3 Marinate the swordfish steaks overnight, after such time they should be opaque.

Cook's Notes

Time
Preparation takes 25 minutes, plus overnight soaking.
Cooking takes about 15 minutes.

Variation
Substitute 2½ tbsps well rinsed canned green peppercorns in place of the fresh peppercorns if you cannot get these, and use tuna steaks instead of the swordfish if you prefer.

Serving Idea
Serve with jacket potatoes and fresh salad.

V Vitamin Content
The fish contains vitamins B and D.

SERVES 4

TARRAGON GRILLED RED SNAPPER

Red snapper is a very decorative little fish that is now readily available at fishmongers and supermarkets.

4 large or 8 small red snapper, cleaned, scaled, washed and dried
4 or 8 sprigs of fresh tarragon
5 tbsps vegetable oil
·2½ tbsps tarragon vinegar
Salt and freshly ground black pepper
1 egg
1¼ tsps Dijon mustard
½ cup sunflower oil
1¼ tbsps wine vinegar
1¼ tsps brandy
1¼ tbsps chopped fresh tarragon
1¼ tbsps chopped fresh parsley
1¼ tbsps heavy cream

1. Rub the inside of each fish with a teaspoonful of salt, scrubbing hard to remove any discolored membranes inside. Rinse thoroughly.

2. Place a sprig of fresh tarragon inside each fish.

3. Using a sharp knife, cut 2 diagonal slits on the side of each fish.

4. Mix together the vegetable oil, tarragon vinegar and a little salt and pepper in a small bowl.

5. Arrange the fish on a shallow dish and pour over the tarragon/vinegar marinade, brushing some of the mixture into the cuts on the side of the fish. Refrigerate for 30 minutes.

6. Put the egg into a blender or food processor along with the mustard and a little salt and pepper. Process for 2-3 seconds to mix.

7 With the machine running, add the oil through the funnel in a thin steady stream. Continue blending the dressing until it is thick and creamy.

8. Add the vinegar, brandy and herbs, and process for a further 30 seconds to mix well.

9. Lightly beat the cream with a small eggbeater until it thickens.

10. Fold the slightly thickened cream carefully into the oil and vinegar dressing. Pour into a serving dish and refrigerate until ready to use.

11. Arrange the fish on a broiler pan and cook under a preheated hot broiler for 5-8 minutes per side, depending on the size of the fish. Baste frequently with the marinade while cooking, then serve with a little of the sauce and some sprigs of fresh tarragon, if you like.

Step 1 Rub the insides of each fish with a teaspoonful of salt, scrubbing briskly to remove any discolored membranes.

Step 3 Using a sharp knife, cut 2 diagonal slits on the side of each fish, taking great care not to cut right through the flesh.

Cook's Notes

Time
Preparation takes about 15 minutes, cooking takes 10-16 minutes.

Variation
Use herrings or mackerel in place of the mullet.

Vitamin Content
All fish is an excellent source of vitamins A and D.

SERVES 4

DUCK WITH ORANGES

This traditional combination is given extra flavor by cooking the duck in a distinctly oriental manner.

3 oranges
1 duck
1 tbsp butter
1¼ tbsps oil
1¼ cups light chicken stock
⅓ cup red wine
2½ tbsps redcurrant jelly
Salt and freshly ground black pepper
1¼ tsps arrowroot
1¼ tbsps cold water

1. Using a potato peeler carefully pare the rind thinly off 2 of the oranges.

Step 2 Using a sharp knife carefully cut the parred orange rind into very thin strips.

2. Cut the rind into very fine shreds using a sharp knife. Put the shredded orange rind into a small bowl and cover with boiling water. Set·aside to blanch for 5 minutes, then drain.

3. Squeeze the juice from the 2 oranges. Set this aside.

4. Cut away the peel and the pith from the remaining orange and then slice the flesh into thin rounds. Set aside.

5. Wash the duck and dry well with paper towels.

6. Put the butter and the oil into a large wok and heat until melted. Add the duck and fry, turning frequently until it is brown all over.

7. Remove the duck from the wok, cool slightly and using poultry shears, cut away the leg and wing ends. Cut the duck in half lengthwise and then cut each half into 1-inch strips.

8. Remove the fat from the wok and return the duck to the wok. Add the stock, red wine, redcurrant jelly, squeezed orange juice, and the well drained strips of rind. Bring to the boil, then season to taste. Reduce the heat, cover the

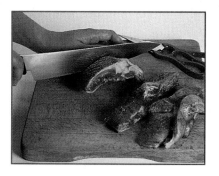

Step 7 Cut each half of the duck into 1-inch strips using poultry shears or a very sharp knife.

wok and simmer the duck gently for 20 minutes, or until well cooked.

9. Skim away any surface fat and thicken the sauce by mixing the arrowroot with the water and stirring into the wok. Bring the mixture back to the boil and simmer for a further 5 minutes, or until the sauce is thick.

10. Arrange the duck on a serving plate and garnish with the orange slices and some additional watercress if liked.

Cook's Notes

Time
Preparation takes 30 minutes, cooking takes 35 minutes.

Serving Idea
Serve with plain boiled rice or sautéed potatoes.

Vitamin Content
Duck is a good source of vitamin B, and oranges are an excellent source of vitamin C.

SERVES 4-6

LIVER WITH ONIONS

This dish is simple to prepare, but absolutely delicious and highly nutritious.

1lb onions
1lb lambs' liver, thinly sliced
Salt and freshly ground black pepper
⅓ cup all-purpose flour
3¾ tbsps vegetable oil
2 tbsps butter
2½ tbsps fresh chopped parsley

1. Peel the onions and slice thinly, keeping each slice in

Step 1 Using a sharp knife, thinly slice the peeled onions, keeping them in rings if possible.

circles if possible.

2. Trim away any large pipes or tubes from the liver using a pair of small scissors or a sharp knife.

3. Mix the seasoning and the flour together on a plate and lay the slices of liver into the flour, turning them and pressing them gently to coat all over evenly.

4. Put the oil and the butter into a large frying pan. Heat

Step 2 Trim away any pipes or tubes from the liver slices using a small pair of scissors or a sharp knife

Step 3 Coat each liver slice thoroughly with the seasoned flour, pressing it gently onto the surface.

gently until foaming.

5. Add the onion rings and fry until just golden.

6. Add the liver slices and fry for 3-5 minutes on each side until well cooked. Cooking time will depend on the thickness of each slice.

7. Stir the parsley into the liver and onions and serve immediately on hot plates.

Cook's Notes

 Time
Preparation takes 15 minutes, cooking takes about 10 minutes.

 Variation
Add 4 oz shredded bacon to this recipe with the onions.

 **Serving Idea**
Serve with creamed potatoes and green vegetables.

Watchpoint
Do not overcook liver or any offal, as it will toughen.

 Freezing
Liver freezes well, but should be frozen before cooking.

 Vitamin Content
Onions are a good source of vitamin C. Liver is an excellent source of vitamins A, B and D.

SERVES 4
'BURNT' CREAM

The gentle cooking of this creamy dessert ensures that the valuable vitamin content in the cream is not decreased in any way.

1¼ cups whole milk
1¼ cups heavy cream
5 egg yolks
⅓ cup superfine sugar
Few drops of vanilla extract
½ cup Barbados sugar
⅔ cup whipped heavy cream (optional)

1. Put the milk and the cream into a heavy-based saucepan and heat gently until almost boiling. Remove from the heat and set aside to cool slightly.

2. Put the egg yolks, sugar and vanilla into a bowl and whip vigorously until they become light and creamy.

3. Strain the milk and cream through a sieve into a large jug.

4. Gradually add the strained milk and cream onto the egg yolk mixture, beating vigorously and constantly as you pour.

5. Rinse the saucepan clean and dry it. Return the egg yolk and cream mixture to the saucepan and heat gently, stirring constantly with a wooden spoon, until the mixture becomes a thick and creamy custard.

6. Do not allow the custard to boil or it will curdle.

7. Strain the custard through a sieve into a shallow serving dish. The custard should come almost to the top of the dish.

8. Stand the custard in a refrigerator and chill until set, preferably overnight.

9. Sprinkle the brown sugar thickly over the surface of the set custard

10. Stand the custard under a preheated hot broiler and cook until the sugar melts and caramelizes. Remove the 'burnt cream' from the broiler and chill it until the sugar layer is a hard, crisp caramel.

11. Serve very cold, decorated with piped heavy cream if desired.

Step 2 Whip the egg yolk, sugar and vanilla together until thick and creamy. The mixture is ready when you can leave a trail on the surface as it is lifted with a spoon or eggbeater.

Step 10 Broil the brown sugar on the top of the chilled custard until it melts and caramelizes.

Cook's Notes

Time
Preparation takes about 15 minutes, cooking takes about 30 minutes, plus chiling time.

Preparation
The custard is ready when the mixture coats the back of a wooden spoon.

Watchpoint
Take great care never to boil the mixture at any stage, or it will curdle. If this should happen, blend 2 tbsps cornstarch with a little milk and stir this into the hot curdled mixture, continue stirring until it thickens and becomes smooth.

Serving Idea
Serve with crisp crackers or a fresh fruit salad.

Vitamin Content
Cream and milk contain vitamins A, B and D. Never expose cream or milk to sunlight, as this will destroy the valuable vitamin B.

SERVES 4
RICE PUDDING

Rice pudding has always been a firm family favorite and this recipe adds spices to make it special enough even for dinner parties.

¼ cup unsalted butter
1 bay leaf, crumbled
1-inch piece cinnamon stick, crushed
1 cup pudding rice, washed and drained
5 cups milk
1¾ cups evaporated milk
¾ cup granulated sugar
½ cup chopped blanched almonds
Seeds of 8 small cardamoms, crushed
¼ cup pistachio nuts, chopped or cut into slivers

1. Melt the butter in a saucepan and fry the bay leaf and cinnamon for 1 minute.

2. Add the rice and stir well to coat evenly with the melted fat.

3. Add the milk and bring the mixture to the boil, then reduce the heat and simmer for 40-50 minutes, stirring occasionally to prevent the rice from sticking to the pan.

4. Add the sugar and the evaporated milk to the rice mixture and continue cooking for a further 20-30 minutes, stirring frequently to prevent burning.

5. It is important to keep stirring the mixture during this cooking time to bring up thin layers of light brown skin which form on the base of the saucepan. This is what gives the pudding its rich, reddish tinge and caramel flavor.

6. Add the chopped almonds and the crushed cardamom seeds to the rice puddings. Stir well and pour into a large serving dish.

7. Decorate the top of the rice pudding with the slivered pistachio nuts, and serve hot or cold.

Step 5 Stir the pudding frequently to bring up the thin layers of light brown skin which will form on the base of the saucepan during cooking.

Step 2 Stir the rice into the fried bay leaf and cinnamon, mixing well to coat each grain evenly with the flavored fat.

Step 7 Decorate the pudding with slivered pistachios before serving.

Cook's Notes

 Time
Preparation takes 10 minutes, cooking takes 1 hour 30 minutes.

 Watchpoint
Frequent stirring is important in this recipe to prevent the sugar from caramelizing too much and giving a bitter flavor to the dessert.

 Vitamin Content
Rice contains vitamins from the B group, and milk and evaporated milk contain vitamins A and D.

SERVES 4-6
SUMMER PUDDING

This favorite summer dessert simply oozes vitamins and flavor.

1½lbs fresh soft fruit, e.g. raspberries, strawberries, rhubarb, redcurrants, blackcurrants or any combination of these fruits
¾ cup granulated sugar
10 thick slices of white bread, crusts removed
1¾ cups fresh cream
1lb fresh whole raspberries

1. Put the 1½lbs of mixed fruit into a large saucepan and stir in the sugar.

2. Heat the fruit gently, shaking the pan vigorously so that the sugar dissolves but the fruit stays as intact as possible. Remove from the heat and cool completely.

3. Cut the slices of bread into thick fingers and use them to line the base and sides of a medium-sized mixing bowl. Press the slices of bread together as firmly as possible to avoid leaving any gaps between them.

4. Pour the cooled fruit and the juice into the center of the pudding, and cover the top completely with the remaining bread. Press down firmly.

5. Place a saucer or small plate over the top of the pudding and weigh this down with cans of food or balance scale weights.

6. Chill the pudding overnight in the refrigerator.

7. Remove the weights and the small plate or saucer. Loosen the sides of the pudding carefully with a round bladed knife, and invert a serving plate over the top of the bowl.

8. Carefully turn both the serving plate and the bowl over, and shake gently. The pudding should drop onto the serving plate.

9. Whip the cream until it is thick, then spread approximately half of the cream over the summer pudding.

Step 2 Shake the fruit and sugar together gently over a low heat until the sugar dissolves, but the fruit remains mainly intact.

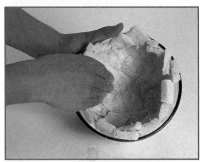

Step 3 Press the slices of bread together well around the sides and the base of the mixing bowl, trying to make sure that there are no gaps in between each slice.

Step 10 Press the whole raspberries into the cream layer covering the summer pudding.

10. Press the fresh raspberries onto the cream in a thick layer all over the pudding, and pipe the remaining cream in small rosettes between the gaps.

11. Chill well, before serving.

Cook's Notes

Time
Preparation takes approximately 30 minutes, plus overnight chiling.

Freezing
This pudding freezes extremely well, but should be decorated with the fruit and cream after it has been thawed.

Vitamin Content
The bread contains vitamin B, the fruit contains vitamin C, and the cream contains vitamin D.

SERVES 4-6

CARROTELLA

Carrots have a natural sweetness which lends itself to sweet as well as savory dishes. Carrotella is a sweet and spicy dessert which should be served very cold.

5 cups milk
1lb carrots, peeled and finely grated
1 cup evaporated milk
½ cup granulated sugar
⅓ cup golden raisins
Seeds of 8 small cardamoms, crushed
2 drops vanilla extract
¼ cup chopped blanched almonds
¼ cup chopped pistachio nuts

1. Put the milk into a saucepan and simmer over a low heat until reduced to about 3½ cups.

2. Add the carrots. Cover and cook over a medium heat for approximately 15 minutes, or until the carrots have begun to soften.

3. Stir in the evaporated milk, sugar and golden raisins, re-cover and simmer gently for about another 5 minutes.

4. Remove the saucepan from the heat, then stir in the crushed cardamom seed and vanilla essence.

5. Beat the carrotella briskly to break up the carrots, then turn into a serving dish and cool slightly.

6. Sprinkle the nuts on top and chill very well before serving.

Step 2 Cook the carrots over a medium heat for 15 minutes, or until they have softened and are breaking up.

Step 6 Sprinkle the partially chilled carrotella with the chopped nuts.

Cook's Notes

Time
Preparation takes 15 minutes. Cooking takes 40 minutes, plus chiling time.

Serving Idea
Serve with a spoonful of chilled fromage frais.

Variation
Use rosewater instead of the vanilla extract, and finely chopped hazelnuts instead of the pistachio nuts.

Vitamin Content
Milk and evaporated milk contain vitamins D and E. Carrots are an excellent source of vitamins A and C.

SERVES 4

BROWN BREAD ICE CREAM

This unusual ice cream is easy to make and is an ideal standby dessert to keep in the freezer.

2 egg yolks
⅓ cup superfine sugar
2 cups heavy or whipping cream
Few drops of vanilla extract
½ cup water
½ cup Barbados sugar
7 tbsps fresh brown breadcrumbs
1¼ tsps ground cinnamon

1. Put the egg yolks and the superfine sugar into a bowl, and whisk vigorously with an electric beater until thick, pale and creamy.

2. Pour in the heavy cream and continue whisking until thick and creamy.

3. Beat in the vanilla extract, then pour the cream mixture into a freezer-proof container and freeze for 1 hour, or until beginning to set around the edges.

4. Break the ice cream away from the edges and whisk with the electric beater until the ice crystals have broken. Return to the freezer and chill for a further hour. Repeat this procedure 2 more times, then freeze completely.

5. Put the water and the brown sugar into a small saucepan and heat gently, stirring until the sugar has dissolved. Bring the mixture to the boil and boil rapidly until the sugar caramelizes.

6. Remove the caramel sugar from the heat and stir in the breadcrumbs and the cinnamon.

7. Spread the caramel mixture onto a cookie sheet lined with oiled wax paper, and allow to set.

8. Break up the caramelized breadcrumbs by placing

Step 1 Whisk the eggs and superfine sugar together until they are pale, thick and creamy.

Step 7 When cooled, the caramelized breadcrumbs should set completely hard.

them in plastic food bags and crushing with a rolling pin.

9. Turn the frozen ice cream into a large bowl and break it up with a fork.

10. Allow the ice cream to soften slightly, then stir in the caramelized breadcrumbs, mixing thoroughly to blend evenly.

11. Return the brown bread ice cream to the freezer tray and freeze completely.

12. Allow the mixture to soften for 10 minutes before serving in scoops.

Cook's Notes

Time
Preparation takes approximately 40 minutes, plus freezing time.

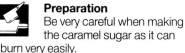

Preparation
Be very careful when making the caramel sugar as it can burn very easily.

V **Vitamin Content**
Wholemeal bread contains vitamins B and E. Fresh cream contains vitamins A, B and D.

SERVES 4-6

FRUITY BREAD PUDDING

This traditional family pudding is made extra nutritious by using whole-wheat bread and a rich assortment of dried fruits.

¾ cup raisins
¾ cup currants
¾ cup golden raisins
¾ cup prunes, stoned and chopped
Finely grated rind and juice of 1 orange
8 thick slices whole-wheat bread, crusts removed
¼ cup butter, softened
½ cup Barbados sugar
1¼ cups whole milk
2 eggs, lightly beaten
½ tsp ground nutmeg
½ tsp ground cinnamon

1. Put all the dried fruit, orange rind and orange juice into a large bowl and mix well.

2. Put about half of the mixed fruit into the base of a lightly buttered ovenproof serving dish.

3. Spread the bread with the butter and cut it into small squares.

4. Arrange half of the bread squares over the fruit in the base of the serving dish.

5. Sprinkle with half of the brown sugar, then repeat the layers once again, finishing with a layer of sugar.

6. Whisk together the milk, eggs, nutmeg and cinnamon. Pour the mixture over the bread pudding and allow to stand for 1 hour.

7. Bake the pudding in a preheated oven, 375°F, for about 35-40 minutes, or until crisp on top but still soft at the bottom. Serve very hot.

Step 5 Arrange the fruit, bread and sugar in layers in an ovenproof dish.

Step 3 Cut the buttered bread into squares approximately 2 inches.

Step 6 Pour the egg and milk mixture over the bread and fruit, taking care not to dislodge the pieces of bread.

Cook's Notes

Time
Preparation takes 15 minutes, plus 1 hour soaking. Cooking takes 40 minutes.

Freezing
This pudding will freeze well and should be reheated for 20 minutes in a hot oven, 375°F. Cover the top with foil to prevent it from burning or browning further.

V

Vitamin Content
Dried fruit is an excellent source of vitamin C, and milk and eggs are good sources of vitamins A, B, D and E. Whole-wheat bread is an excellent source of vitamins B and E.

SERVES 4

CARAMEL ORANGES

Rich in vitamins A and C, oranges need very little preparation to provide a delicious dessert.

4 large oranges
1½ cups granulated sugar
1¼ cups water
4 tbsps boiling water
2½ tbsps Cointreau

Step 1 Cut the parred orange rind into very thin julienne strips with a sharp knife.

1. Using a potato peeler or very sharp knife, carefully pare the peel only from the oranges. Cut this peel into very thin strips, removing any white pith as you do so.

2. Put the orange peel strips into a small bowl and cover with boiling water. Allow to stand for 20 minutes, then drain.

3. Carefully peel all the pith from the oranges with a serrated edged knife. Cut the oranges horizontally into slices approximately ¼-inch thick. Reserve any juice which spills in a small jug.

Step 3 Carefully remove all the white pith from the oranges, using a serrated knife and cutting with a sawing action.

4. Put the orange juice, the 1¼ cups water and sugar into a small saucepan, and heat gently all the time until the sugar has dissolved.

5. Increase the temperature and bring the sugar syrup to the boil, boiling rapidly until it turns a pale gold color.

6. Remove the caramel from the heat and quickly stir in the 4 tbsps of boiling water.

Step 5 Cook the sugar and the syrup over a moderate heat, until it turns pale gold in color. Take care not to overcook at this stage.

7. Add the orange rind to the sugar syrup along with the Cointreau, and allow to cool completely.

8. Arrange the orange slices in a serving dish, and pour over the cooled syrup. Chill for several hours or overnight, before serving.

Cook's Notes

Time
Preparation takes 25 minutes, cooking takes 20 minutes.

Watchpoint
Take care not to overcook the sugar syrup or it will burn and spoil the flavor.

Preparation
Hold the pan slightly away from you when adding the boiling water, as the syrup will splutter and spit and can give a very nasty burn.

Freezing
Fresh oranges freeze very well, but sugar syrup should be made fresh each time.

V Vitamin Content
Oranges are an excellent source of vitamins A and C.

MAKES 1 x 10-INCH LOAF

CARROT CAKE

Carrots give a cake a delicious sweet flavor, as well as lots of vitamins and minerals. What better excuse do you need to indulge in this delicious tea-time treat.

¾ cup butter
¾ cup Barbados sugar
2 eggs, well beaten
2 cups all-purpose whole-wheat flour
2 tsps baking soda
¾ tsp baking powder
½ tsp ground cinnamon
½ tsp ground nutmeg
¾ tsp salt
½lb peeled carrots, grated
⅔ cup raisins
½ cup finely chopped walnuts
½ tsp cardamom seeds, crushed
Confectioners' sugar, for dredging

1. Beat the butter and sugar together until they are light and fluffy.

2. Add the eggs a little at a time, beating well and adding a teaspoonful of the flour with each addition, to prevent the mixture from curdling.

3. Put the remaining flour into a large bowl along with the bicarbonate of soda, baking powder, cinnamon, nutmeg and salt. Mix together well.

4. Carefully fold the flour into the butter and egg mixture, mixing well to ensure that it is blended evenly.

5. Add the carrots, raisins, nuts and cardamom seeds, beating the mixture well to blend evenly.

6. Lightly grease a 10-inch loaf pan and line the base with a piece of silicone paper.

7. Pour the cake mixture into the loaf pan, and bake in a preheated oven 350°F, for 45-50 minutes or until a fine metal skewer comes out clean when inserted into the center of the cake.

8. Cool the cake in its pan for 15 minutes before turning out onto a wire rack to cool completely.

9. Dredge the cake with confectioners' sugar just before serving.

Step 2 Beat the eggs gradually into the butter and sugar, adding a little flour with each addition to prevent the mixture from curdling.

Step 5 Stir the carrots, fruit and nuts into the cake mixture, mixing well to blend evenly.

Cook's Notes

Time
Preparation takes 30 minutes, cooking takes 45-50 minutes.

Watchpoint
If the egg and butter mixture should curdle, add a little more flour and beat very hard with an electric whisk until the curdling disappears.

Vitamin Content
Whole-wheat flour is an excellent source of vitamins B and D. Carrots are an excellent source of vitamins A and C.

MAKES 1 x 8-INCH CAKE

TOASTED ALMOND CAKE

A crunchy toasted almond topping makes this cake very different from run-of-the-mill tea-time treats.

⅔ cup butter, softened
½ cup superfine sugar
2 eggs, lightly beaten
1½ cups whole-wheat self-rising flour
¾ tsp vanilla extract
2½ tbsps orange juice
⅓ cup Barbados sugar
¼ cup melted, unsalted butter
1¼ tbsps milk
½ cup slivered almonds
½ cup confectioners' sugar
2½ tbsps cornstarch
3 egg yolks
½ cup milk
⅓ cup heavy cream, whipped
½ tsp almond extract

1. Beat the butter and superfine sugar until it is light and fluffy.

2. Beat in the eggs one at a time, adding a teaspoonful of the flour with each addition to prevent the mixture from curdling.

3. Fold in all the remaining flour, along with the vanilla extract and the orange juice.

4. Lightly grease a 8-inch cake pan, and line the base with a piece of silicone paper.

5. Spoon the cake mixture into the pan and spread the top evenly with a palette knife.

6. Put the brown sugar into a small saucepan, along with the melted butter, the 1¼ tbsps milk and the slivered almonds. Stir over a low heat until the sugar has completely dissolved.

7. Sprinkle about 1¼ tbsps of additional flour over the top of the cake mixture in the pan, then pour over the melted sugar, butter and almond mixture. Spread it evenly, but try not to disturb the cake mixture too much.

8. Bake the cake in a preheated oven 375°F for 20-30 minutes, or until the cake is well risen and the topping has caramelized golden brown.

9. Put the confectioners' sugar, cornstarch and egg yolks into a bowl, and using an electric beater, whisk until they are light and fluffy.

10. Pour on the milk, gradually whisking between additions. Strain this egg yolk mixture through a sieve into a heavy-based saucepan.

11. Cook the egg yolk and milk mixture over a gentle heat until it begins to thicken, and will thickly coat the back of a wooden spoon. Stir the mixture frequently during the cooking time to prevent it from burning or curdling.

12. Remove from the heat and cool.

13. When the custard is completely cool, lightly fold in the cream and the almond extract.

14. When the cake has cooled, carefully cut it in half horizontally with a sharp knife. Sandwich the two halves back together using the almond custard as a filling.

15. Chill thoroughly before serving.

Cook's Notes

Time
Preparation takes 40 minutes. Cooking takes about 30 minutes, plus 10 minutes for the filling.

Watchpoint
Do not allow the almond topping to become too hot. Heat it just long enough to dissolve the sugar. If it does overheat, allow it to cool before pouring onto the uncooked cake mixture.

Vitamin Content
Whole-wheat flour contains B group vitamins and vitamin E. Nuts contain vitamins B and E, and butter and eggs contain vitamins A, B, D and E. Milk and cream contain vitamins A and D.

MAKES 1 x 8-INCH CAKE

CINNAMON BUTTER CREAM CAKE

This sumptuous cake has the added advantage of requiring no cooking.

1⅓ cup granulated sugar
¾ tsp ground cinnamon
7½ tbsps water
8 egg yolks
2 cups unsalted butter, softened
48 ladyfingers
10 tbsps brandy
1 cup toasted almonds, roughly chopped
1 cup unsweetened chocolate, coarsely grated

Step 9 Line the cake pan with trimmed ladyfingers and spread with approximately half of the buttercream.

1. Put the sugar, water and cinnamon in a small heavy-based saucepan and bring to the boil, stirring constantly until the sugar dissolves.

2. Allow the sugar syrup to boil briskly without stirring, until it begins to thicken, but has not browned. This temperature should be 236°F on a sugar thermometer; or when the sugar mixture will form a small ball when dropped into a bowl of cold water.

3. Beat the egg yolks in a large bowl with an electric mixer, until they are pale and thick.

4. Pour the sugar syrup quickly, in a thin steady stream, into the whisked egg yolks, beating constantly with the electric beater.

5. Continue beating in this way until the mixture is thick, smooth and creamy. Allow to cool at room temperature.

6. Still using the electric mixer, beat the softened butter a spoonful at a time, into the egg and sugar mixture. Beat well to ensure that it is evenly distributed. Chill the mixture until it reaches spreading consistency.

7. Line an 8-inch square pan with greased foil or silicone paper.

8. Cut the ladyfingers into neat pieces to enable you to use them to line the cake pan.

9. Divide the butter cream in half and spread a little of the buttercream lightly on one side of each biscuit and place them, icing side down, into the pan.

10. Cut any small pieces of biscuits to fill any corners, if necessary.

11. Continue spreading the buttercream on the ladyfingers and lining the cake pan in this way, alternating the direction of the fingers between the layers.

12. Sprinkle half of the brandy over the ladyfingers, then continue spreading the remainder of the sponge with just half of the buttercream and filling the cake pan completely. Sprinkle with the remaining brandy, then chill in the refrigerator overnight.

13. Remove the cake from the pan and peel off the paper or foil. Slide the cake onto a flat surface and coat with the remaining half of the buttercream.

14. Press the chopped almonds on to the sides of the cake and decorate the top with the grated chocolate. Serve immediately, or chill in the refrigerator until required.

Cook's Notes

Time
Preparation takes about 45 minutes, plus overnight chiling.

Freezing
This cake freezes well.

Variation
The icing may be flavored with 2 tsps instant coffee powder, which should be added when making the syrup.

Vitamin Content
Butter contains vitamins A, B and D, and eggs contain vitamins B and E. Nuts contain vitamins B and E.

LOW
CALORIE

Introduction

Keeping a check on your weight is probably one of the best ways to improve your general health. By eating a nutritionally balanced, calorie-controlled diet you will be helping your body to become fitter and to function more efficiently. Being overweight increases the chances of high blood pressure, thrombosis and heart attack, it makes keeping fit more difficult and often leaves people with low self-esteem. This is not to suggest that we should all be "model-girl slim." Watching your weight simply means sustaining a healthy weight for your height and age.

Whether you are on a weight-reducing diet or are simply trying to sustain your present weight, it is important to balance the food you consume against the benefits obtained from it. A chocolate milkshake will provide you with a few important nutrients, but it will not provide you with sufficient amounts of fiber, vitamins or protein for one meal, nor will it educate you to rely upon a well balanced and regular diet.

Calorie counting is in fact an ideal way of checking, on a daily basis, that you are consuming the correct amount of calories to stay at your present weight. If the amount of calories being consumed does not exceed the amount of calories being expended, a constant body weight will be maintained. In this respect the significance of regular exercise cannot be ignored – the more active you are the easier weight control becomes. There are no fast solutions to maintaining a healthy weight, a nutritionally balanced, calorie-controlled diet in conjunction with regular exercise is the healthiest and most natural answer.

These recipes have been compiled to help you plan a regular pattern of eating which is both low in calories and high in enjoyment. All the recipes are calorie counted so all you have to do is set a realistic daily allowance and decide which of the easily prepared meals to include in your menu.

SERVES 4
44 kilocalories per serving

CARROT SOUP

Carrots make a most delicious soup which is both filling and extremely low in calories.

1lb carrots
1 medium-sized onion
1 medium-sized turnip
2 cloves garlic, minced
3 cups water or vegetable stock
¾ tsp dried thyme
¾ tsp ground nutmeg
Salt and ground white pepper to taste
Toasted sunflower seeds, slivered almonds and pistachio nuts, mixed together for garnish

1. Peel the carrots and cut them into thick slices.

2. Peel and roughly chop the onion and turnip.

3. Put the vegetables, garlic and water or stock, into a large saucepan and bring to the boil. Cover the pan, reduce the heat and simmer for 20 minutes.

4. Add all the seasonings and simmer for a further 5 minutes.

5. Remove the soup from the heat and allow to cool for 15 minutes.

6. Using a liquidizer or food processor, blend the soup until it is thick and smooth.

7. Reheat the soup as required, garnishing with the seeds and nuts before serving.

Step 2 Using a sharp knife, roughly chop the peeled onions and turnip.

Step 1 Cut the carrots into thick slices, approximately ½-inch thick.

Step 6 Purée the soup in a liquidizer or food processor, until it is thick and smooth.

Cook's Notes

Time
Preparation takes about 12 minutes, cooking takes 25-30 minutes.

Cook's Tip
Make the recipe in double quantities and freeze half for a future date.

Variation
Use ¼ tsp cayenne pepper in place of the nutmeg in this recipe.

SERVES 4

115 kilocalories per serving

MELON AND PROSCIUTTO

This typically Italian appetizer is wonderful served well chilled on warm summer days.

1 large ripe melon, either Galia or Honeydew
16 thin slices prosciutto ham
French flat leaf parsley to garnish

Step 1 Using a spoon, scoop out and discard the seeds and fibrous core of the melon.

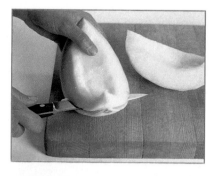

Step 2 Carefully remove the rind from the quartered melon, using a sharp knife.

Step 4 Roll a slice of prosciutto ham around each thin slice of melon.

1. Cut the melon in half lengthwise. Using a spoon, scoop out and discard all the seeds and fibers.

2. Cut the melon into quarters and carefully peel away the skin using a sharp knife.

3. Cut each quarter into 4 thin slices.

4. Wrap each slice of melon in a slice of the prosciutto ham, and arrange on a serving dish. Chill well and garnish with parsley before serving.

Cook's Notes

Time
Preparation takes 15 minutes.

Cook's Tip
Use this recipe, along with other items such as olives, stuffed eggs and sliced salami, as Italian antipasta for a buffet party.

Variation
Serve the slices of prosciutto ham in rolls, accompanied by quartered fresh figs in place of the melon.

SERVES 20

334 kilocalories per serving

SPICED BEEF

Spiced beef makes an attractive addition to a buffet or cold table and only a small serving is necessary for each guest. If you do not wish to cook a piece of meat this size, simply reduce the recipe by half.

6lb piece brisket, silverside, or topside of beef
3 bay leaves
1¼ tsps powdered mace
6 cloves
1¼ tsps black peppercorns
1¼ tsps allspice
2 large cloves garlic
2½ tbsps molasses
2½ tbsps brown sugar
1lb cooking salt
2¼ tsps saltpetre

1. Trim the excess fat from the piece of beef and make sure that it is well tied with string, so that it will keep its shape during the spicing.

2. Break the bay leaves into small pieces, and mix with the powdered mace.

3. Put the cloves, peppercorns and allspice into a mortar and crush them to a fine powder with a pestle.

4. Chop the garlic and add this to the crushed spices in the mortar, along with 1 tsp of the salt. Blend this to a paste, using the pestle.

5. Put the bay leaves, mace, ground spices, garlic, black treacle, brown sugar, cooking salt and the saltpetre in a very large bowl, and mix them together thoroughly.

6. Place the beef in a bowl, and rub all the surfaces thoroughly with the spicing mixture. Cover the bowl and set aside.

7. Repeat this process every day for 1 week, turning the meat and rubbing in the spices each day. Keep the meat in a cool place, or refrigerator, during this time.

8. To cook, cover the joint of beef with water in a very large saucepan. Bring the water to the boil, cover and simmer slowly for 6 hours. Allow the meat to cool in the cooking liquid.

9. Remove the cooled meat from the liquid, remove the string and place in a tight fitting dish or large loaf pan.

10. Put a plate on top of the piece of beef and weigh it down with balance scale weights or bags of sugar. Leave the beef to press in a cool place overnight.

11. To serve, slice the beef very thinly and serve cold on a bed of lettuce.

Step 6 Rub the surface of the beef evenly with some of the spicing mixture, making sure that all surface areas are well coated.

Step 8 Put the beef in a large pan and pour over enough water to cover.

Cook's Notes

Time
Preparation takes 1 week, cooking time takes approximately 6 hours.

Cook's Tip
Saltpetre can be purchased from any chemist.

Watchpoint
Make sure the beef in kept in a cool place whilst the spicing takes effect.

SERVES 4

24 kilocalories per serving

ORANGE, GRAPEFRUIT AND MINT SALAD

Fresh citrus fruits are complemented beautifully by the fragrant flavor of fresh mint. Serve chilled for an ideal low calorie appetizer.

2 grapefruits
3 oranges
Liquid sweetener to taste (optional)
8 sprigs of mint

1. Using a serrated knife, cut away the peel and the white pith from the grapefruit and the oranges.

2. Carefully cut inside the skin of each segment to remove each section of flesh.

3. Squeeze the membranes over a bowl to extract all the juice. Sweeten the juice with the liquid sweetener, if required.

4. Arrange the orange and the grapefruit segments in alternating colors on 4 individual serving dishes.

5. Using a sharp knife, chop 4 springs of the mint very finely. Stir the chopped mint into the fruit juice.

6. Carefully spoon the juice over the arranged fruit segments and chill thoroughly.

7. Garnish with a sprig of mint before serving.

Step 1 Using a serrated knife, cut away the peel from the grapefruits and the oranges, making sure that you remove all the white pith as you cut.

Step 2 Carefully cut inside the skin of each segment to remove each section of flesh, trying to keep each piece as intact as possible.

Cook's Notes

Time
Preparation takes about 20 minutes, plus chiling time.

Cook's Tip
This appetizer can be prepared up to a day in advance.

Preparation
Make sure all the white pith is removed from the fruit, as it produces a bitter flavor.

Variation
Use ruby grapefruits and blood oranges, when available, in place of the normal types of fruit for a colorful variation. Use borage leaves in place of the mint, and garnish with a few of the blue flowers.

SERVES 4
41 kilocalories per serving

INDIAN TOMATO SOUP

This highly fragrant and spicy tomato soup makes an interesting low calorie appetizer.

½lb tomatoes
1 medium-sized onion
2½ tbsps vegetable oil
1 green chili, seeded and finely chopped
3 cloves garlic, minced
1¼ tbsps tomato paste
4½ cups water, or vegetable stock
4-6 green curry leaves, or ¾ tsp curry powder
Freshly ground sea salt to taste
Coriander leaves and green chilies for garnish

1. Cut a small cross in the skin of each tomato and plunge them into boiling water for 30-40 seconds.

2. Remove the tomatoes and carefully peel away the loosened skin with a sharp knife.

3. Remove the green core from the tomatoes and roughly chop the flesh.

4. Peel the onion and chop it into small pieces using a sharp knife.

5. Heat the oil in a large saucepan and gently sauté the onion, chopped chili and garlic for 3-4 minutes until it is soft, but not browned.

6. Stir in the chopped tomatoes and cook for 5 minutes, stirring often to prevent the vegetables from burning.

7. Blend the tomato paste with the water and pour this into the onions and tomatoes. Add the curry leaves or powder, season with the salt and simmer for 5-7 minutes.

8. Remove the soup from the heat and stir in the coriander leaves and the chili halves.

9. Pour the soup into 4-6 serving bowls and serve piping hot, discarding the chili garnish before eating.

Step 2 Remove the tomatoes from the boiling water and carefully peel away the loosened skin.

Step 3 Cut away and discard the hard green core from the tomatoes, and chop the flesh roughly with a sharp knife.

 Cook's Notes

 Time
Preparation takes about 15 minutes, cooking takes 17-18 minutes.

! **Watchpoint**
Great care must be taken when preparing fresh chilies. Try not to get the juice into your eyes or mouth. If this should happen, rinse with lots of cold water.

 Freezing
This soup freezes well, but should be frozen before adding the garnish.

SERVES 4
113 kilocalories per serving
"BURNT" PEPPER SALAD

Burning peppers under a hot broiler is a traditional way of preparing this sweet vegetable which enhances, rather than impairs, its subtle flavor.

3 large colored peppers, e.g. red, green and yellow
5 tbsps olive oil
1 clove garlic, finely chopped
8 basil leaves, roughly chopped
3 sprigs of fresh marjoram, roughly chopped
2½ tbsps fresh pickled capers
2½ tbsps white wine vinegar

1. Cut the peppers in half lengthwise. Remove and discard the core and seeds.

Step 2 Press the pepper halves down on a flat surface with the palm of your hands to flatten them completely.

2. Lay the peppers, cut side down, on a flat surface and flatten them out by pressing down with the palm of your hand.

3. Preheat the broiler to hot. Arrange the peppers on a broiler pan and brush with 1¼ tbsps of the olive oil.

4. Broil the peppers until the skins are well charred. Wrap them in a clean towel and leave for 15 minutes.

5. Unwrap the peppers and peel off the charred and

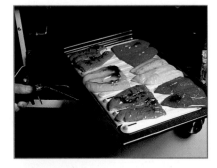

Step 4 Char the skin of the peppers under a hot broiler, turning them around, if necessary, to burn evenly.

Step 5 Wrap the charred peppers in a cloth to retain the moisture and lift the charred skins away from the pepper flesh.

loosened skin.

6. Cut the peppers into thick strips and arrange them onto a serving dish.

7. Scatter over the chopped garlic, basil leaves, marjoram and capers.

8. Mix together the remaining olive oil and the vinegar, and pour over the peppers. Refrigerate for at least 1 hour before serving.

Cook's Notes

Time
Preparation takes about 30 minutes, plus 1 hour chiling time.

Variation
For a special occasion use nasturtium flower buds instead of the capers.

Preparation
The skins of the peppers must be very well charred on the outside before wrapping them in the towel, otherwise their skin will not peel away properly.

Cook's Tip
If you do not wish to broil the peppers, pierce the whole pepper with a fork and hold them over a gas flame to char the skin.

SERVES 2
252 kilocalories per serving

FRESH TOMATO OMELET

Omelets can make substantial low calorie lunches or light meals and can be varied by using different fillings. This recipe uses lots of tasty fresh tomatoes, which can be eaten in abundance on a calorie controlled diet.

1lb fresh tomatoes
Salt and freshly ground black pepper
4 eggs
5 tbsps water
¾ tsp fresh chopped basil
2½ tbsps olive or vegetable oil
¾ tsp fresh chopped oregano or basil to garnish

1. Cut a small cross into the skins of each tomato and plunge them into boiling water. Leave for 30 seconds, then remove them with a draining spoon.

2. Using a sharp knife carefully peel away the tomato skins and discard them.

3. Cut the tomatoes in half and remove and discard the seeds, juice and any tough core.

4. Cut the tomato flesh into thin strips.

5. Break the eggs into a bowl and beat in the water and chopped herbs. Season with salt and pepper and continue beating until the egg mixture is frothy.

6. Heat the oil in a large frying pan or skillet, then pour in the egg mixture.

7. Using a spatula, stir the egg mixture around the skillet for about 2-3 minutes, or until the eggs are beginning to set.

8. Spread the tomato strips over the partially cooked eggs, and continue cooking without stirring until the eggs have completely set and the tomatoes are just warmed through.

9. Sprinkle with the additional chopped basil before serving.

Step 2 Carefully peel away and discard the tomato skins from the blanched fruit, using a sharp knife.

Step 3 Remove the seeds and juice from the halved tomatoes with a teaspoon.

Step 5 Beat the eggs, water and herbs together thoroughly, until they are frothy.

Cook's Notes

Time
Preparation takes about 25 minutes, cooking takes about 5 minutes.

Variation
Add 1 clove of minced garlic to the egg mixture, if desired.

Serving Idea
Cut the omelet into wedges and serve straight from the frying pan.

SERVES 4

83 kilocalories per serving

VEGETABLE KEBABS

A colorful and flavorsome way to serve delicious fresh vegetables as part of a low calorie diet.

1 large eggplant
Salt
1 large green pepper
4 zucchini
12-14 cherry tomatoes, red or yellow
12-14 pickling onions
12-14 button mushrooms
5 tbsps olive oil
2½ tbsps lemon juice
¾ tsp salt
¾ tsp freshly ground black pepper

1. Cut the eggplant in half and dice it into 1-inch pieces.

2. Put the eggplant pieces into a large bowl, and sprinkle liberally with salt. Stir well and allow to stand for 30 minutes to degorge.

3. Rinse the eggplant pieces thoroughly in a colander under cold water, to remove all traces of salt.

4. Cut the green pepper in half. Remove and discard the core and seeds. Cut the pepper flesh into 1-inch pieces with a sharp knife.

5. Slice the zucchini diagonally into pieces approximately 1-inch thick.

6. Remove the tough cores form the cherry tomatoes and peel the onions. Rinse the mushrooms under cold water to remove any bits of soil, but do not peel.

7. Put all the prepared vegetables into a large bowl and pour in the remaining ingredients. Mix well to coat evenly, cover with plastic wrap and allow to stand for about 30 minutes, stirring the vegetables once or twice to ensure they remain evenly coated.

8. Thread the vegetables alternately onto skewers and arrange them on a broiler pan.

9. Brush the kebabs with the marinade and broil for 3-4 minutes, turning frequently and basting with the marinade until they are evenly browned. Serve piping hot.

Step 5 Cut the zucchini diagonally into 1-inch pieces.

Step 8 Thread the prepared and marinated vegetables alternately onto kebab skewers, keeping an even number of vegetable pieces on each skewer.

Cook's Notes

Time
Preparation takes about 30 minutes. Cooking takes about 10 minutes, plus time for the vegetables to marinate.

Preparation
It is important to degorge the eggplant before cooking, as this removes the bitterness from the flavor and some of the moisture as well.

Variation
Use any combination of your favorite vegetables in this recipe.

SERVES 6

213 kilocalories per serving

DOLMAS

Delicious individual parcels of rice, herbs, nuts and fruit, make a very different low calorie lunch or supper dish.

12 large cabbage leaves, washed
1 cup long grain rice
8 green onions
1¼ tbsps fresh chopped basil
1¼ tbsps fresh chopped mint
1¼ tbsps fresh chopped parsley
½ cup pine nuts
⅓ cup currants
Salt and freshly ground black pepper
5 tbsps olive oil
Juice 1 lemon
⅔ cup unset natural yogurt
¼lb cucumber

Step 5 Pile tablespoons of the filling onto the blanched leaves, pressing it gently into sausage shapes in the center of the leaves.

1. Using a sharp knife trim away any tough stems from the cabbage leaves.

2. Put the leaves into boiling water for about 30 seconds. Remove them using a slotted spoon and drain thoroughly before laying them out flat on a work surface.

3. Put the rice into a saucepan along with enough boiling water to just cover. Cook for 15-20 minutes, or until the rice is soft and the liquid almost completely absorbed. Rinse the rice in cold water to remove any starchiness.

4. Cut the green onions into thin diagonal slices. Put the rice and the chopped onions into a large bowl along with all the remaining ingredients, except 2½ tbsps olive oil, the yogurt and cucumber. Mix the rice mixture thoroughly to blend evenly.

5. Place about 2 tbsps of the rice filling onto each blanched cabbage leaf, pressing it gently into a sausage shape.

6. Fold the sides of the leaves over to partially cover the stuffing, and then roll up, jelly roll fashion, to completely envelop the filling.

7. Place the rolls seam side down in a large baking dish. Brush with the remaining olive oil. Pour hot water around the cabbage leaves until it comes about halfway up their sides.

8. Cover the baking dish with aluminum foil, pressing it gently onto the surface of the leaves to keep them in place. Bake in a preheated oven 375°F for 30-40 minutes.

9. Peel the cucumber and cut it lengthwise into quarters. Remove the pips and discard. Chop the cucumber flesh and half of the peel into very small pieces.

10. Mix the chopped cucumber into the yogurt and chill until required.

11. Drain the dolmas from the cooking liquid and arrange on a serving plate with a little of the cucumber sauce spooned over.

Cook's Notes

Time
Preparation takes about 30 minutes, cooking takes 40 minutes.

Serving Idea
Serve the dolmas either hot or cold.

Preparation
Dolmas can be prepared a day in advance and allowed to stand in their liquid in the refrigerator. They can be reheated just before serving if required.

Variation
Use any other ingredients you particularly like in the filling along with the rice. Use vine leaves instead of cabbage leaves in this recipe.

SERVES 6
156 kilocalories per serving
EGGPLANT BAKE

Eggplants are wonderfully filling vegetables with very few calories – the ideal ingredient in a calorie controlled diet.

2 large or 3 medium-sized eggplants
2½ tsps salt
⅔ cup malt vinegar
2½ tbsps vegetable oil
2 large onions, peeled and sliced into rings
2 green chilies, seeded and finely chopped
2 cups peeled plum tomatoes, chopped
¾ tsp chili powder
1¼ tsps minced garlic
¾ tsp ground turmeric
8 tomatoes, sliced
1⅓ cups natural unset yogurt
1¼ tsps freshly ground black pepper
1 cup Cheddar cheese, finely grated

1. Cut the eggplants into ¼-inch thick slices. Arrange the slices in a shallow dish and sprinkle with 1½ tsps of the salt. Pour over the malt vinegar, cover the dish and marinate for 30 minutes.

2. Drain the eggplant well, discarding the marinade liquid.

3. Heat the vegetable oil in a frying pan and gently fry the onion rings until they are golden brown.

4. Add the chilies, the remaining salt, chopped tomatoes, chili powder, garlic and turmeric. Mix well and simmer for 5-7 minutes until thick and well blended.

5. Remove the sauce from the heat and cool slightly. Blend to a smooth purée using a liquidizer or food processor.

6. Arrange half of the eggplant slices in the base of a lightly greased shallow ovenproof dish.

7. Spoon half of the tomato sauce over the eggplant slices. Cover the tomato sauce with the remaining eggplant, and then top this with the remaining tomato sauce and sliced tomatoes.

8. Mix together the yogurt, the freshly ground black pepper and the Cheddar cheese. Pour this mixture over the tomato slices.

9. Preheat an oven to 375°F, and cook the eggplant bake for 20-30 minutes, or until the cheese topping bubbles and turns golden brown. Serve hot straight from the oven.

Step 4 Fry the chilies, tomatoes and seasoning with the golden onion rings until they are softened and juice flows.

Step 7 Spoon half the tomato sauce over the eggplant slices in the gratin dish.

Cook's Notes

Time
Preparation takes about 30 minutes, cooking takes 40 minutes.

Preparation
Make sure that the eggplants are well drained when they are removed from the marinade. Press them into a colander using the back of your hand, to remove all excess vinegar. Do not rinse, as the vinegar gives a tangy flavor to the dish.

Cook's Tip
Use a low calorie cheese in place of the Cheddar cheese to reduce the calorie content further.

SERVES 4

54 kilocalories per serving

OKRA CASSEROLE

Okra has an interesting texture and a mild flavor which combines well with tomatoes to make this delicious Mediterranean-style casserole.

2½ tbsps olive oil
1 small onion
½lb fresh okra
6 ripe tomatoes
Juice of ½ lemon
Salt and freshly ground black pepper
2½ tbsps fresh chopped parsley

---

1. Peel the onions and cut them in half lengthwise. Use a sharp knife to cut them across in slices.

2. Heat the oil in a large saucepan and cook the onion until it is soft and transparent, but not browned.

3. Remove just the stems from the okra, but leave on the pointed tail. Take care not to cut off the very top of the okra.

4. Add the okra to the onions and cook gently for 10 minutes, stirring occasionally.

5. Cut a small cross into the skins of the tomatoes, and

plunge them into boiling water for 30 seconds.

6. Drain the tomatoes and carefully peel away and discard the loosened skins. Chop the peeled fruit roughly.

7. Add the tomatoes, lemon juice, seasoning and parsley to the okra, and continue to cook for about 5 more minutes, or until the tomatoes are just heated through.

8. Spoon into a serving dish and serve hot or cold.

Step 3 Trim just the stems from the top of the okra, but take care not to remove the whole top, or the pointed tails.

Step 1 Place the halved peeled onions cut side downwards, and use a sharp knife to cut across into thin slices.

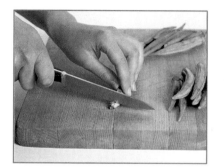

Step 6 Carefully peel the skins away from the blanched tomatoes, using a sharp knife.

Cook's Notes

Time
Preparation takes 15 minutes, cooking takes approximately 15 minutes.

Variation
Green beans can be used in place of the okra.

Cook's Tip
If you cannot get fresh okra, use canned okra in its place, but drain and rinse this before use and cut the cooking time in half.

Watchpoint
If too much liquid is left at the end of cooking, remove the vegetables with a slotted spoon and boil the liquid quickly to reduce the sauce.

SERVES 6

234 kilocalories per serving

PASTA WITH FRESH TOMATO AND BASIL SAUCE

Pasta is a good item to include on a low calorie diet, as it is very filling and can be served with any variety of low calorie sauces.

1 small onion, finely chopped
1lb fresh tomatoes
2½ tbsps tomato paste
1 orange
2 cloves garlic, minced
Salt and freshly ground black pepper
⅔ cup red wine
⅔ cup chicken stock
2½ tbsps coarsely chopped basil
1¾ cups whole-wheat pasta

1. Peel and finely chop the onion.

2. Cut a small cross in the skins of the tomatoes and plunge them into boiling water for 30 seconds. Remove the blanched tomatoes from the water and carefully peel away the loosened skin.

3. Cut the tomatoes into quarters, and remove and discard the pips. Chop the tomato flesh roughly, and put this, the onion and the tomato paste into a large saucepan.

4. Heat the onion and tomatoes over a gentle heat, stirring continuously until the tomatoes soften and begin to lose their juice.

5. Finely grate the rind from the orange. Cut the orange in half and squeeze out the juice.

6. Put the orange, rind and juice into a large saucepan along with all the remaining ingredients, and bring to the boil.

Step 1 To chop an onion finely, pierce the peeled onion with a fork and use this to hold the vegetable steady whilst you chop with a sharp knife.

Step 3 Cut the tomatoes into quarters and remove and discard the seeds.

7. Continue to boil until the sauce has reduced and thickened and the vegetables are soft.

8. Whilst the sauce is cooking, put the pasta into another saucepan with enough boiling water to cover. Season with a little salt and cook for 10-15 minutes, or until the pasta is soft.

9. Drain the pasta in a colander, and stir it into the hot sauce. Serve at once with a salad.

Cook's Notes

Time
Preparation takes 15-20 minutes, cooking takes 10-15 minutes.

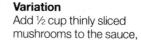

Variation
Add ½ cup thinly sliced mushrooms to the sauce, if liked.

Freezing
This sauce will freeze very well for up to 3 months.

SERVES 6
153 kilocalories per serving

VEGETABLE AND OLIVE CASSEROLE

The addition of vinegar and capers gives this refreshing vegetable dish a sharp twist to its flavor.

1 eggplant
Salt
⅔ cup olive, or vegetable oil
1 onion, peeled and thinly sliced
2 red peppers, seeded and chopped
2 sticks of celery, sliced thickly
1lb canned plum tomatoes
2½ tbsps red wine vinegar
1¼ tbsps sugar
1 clove garlic, minced
12 black olives, pitted
1¼ tbsps capers
Salt and freshly ground black pepper

1. Cut the eggplant in half lengthwise and score the cut surface deeply, in a lattice fashion, with the point of a sharp knife.

2. Sprinkle the cut surface of the eggplant liberally with salt, and leave to stand for 30 minutes.

3. Rinse the eggplants thoroughly under running water, then pat dry and cut it into 1-inch cubes.

4. Heat the oil in a large sauté pan and add the onion, peppers and celery. Cook gently for about 5 minutes, stirring occasionally until the vegetables have softened but not browned.

5. Add the eggplant to the pan and mix well to coat thoroughly with the oil. Continue cooking gently for 5 minutes.

6. Chop the plum tomatoes and then press them through a nylon sieve, using the back of a wooden spoon to press out all the juice and pulp, leaving the seeds and pith in the sieve.

7. Add the sieved tomatoes to the vegetables in the sauté pan, along with the remaining ingredients, except for the olives and capers. Cover and simmer for 5 minutes.

8. Cut the olives into quarters and add these to the simmering vegetables, along with the capers.

9. Continue cooking gently, uncovered, for a further 15 minutes, or until most of the liquid has evaporated and the sauce has thickened and reduced.

Step 1 Score the cut surface of the eggplants in a lattice pattern, using the point of a sharp knife.

Step 9 Simmer the casserole, uncovered, over a low heat until the juice has thickened and reduced.

Cook's Notes

Time
Preparation takes 30 minutes, plus 30 minutes for the eggplants to degorge. Cooking takes approximately 25 minutes.

Preparation
Scoring and salting the eggplant will remove any bitter taste and toughness from the vegetable. Be very sure, however, to rinse all the salt off the eggplant before cooking, or this will affect the flavor of the dish.

Cook's Tip
This recipe may be prepared 2-3 days in advance and kept covered in a refrigerator.

Serving Idea
This recipe is delicious served cold as a salad, or hot with rice and pitta bread.

SERVES 6
21 kilocalories per serving

SALADE PAYSANNE

This homely salad can be made with any selection of fresh vegetables you have to hand. So whether its winter or summer, there's no excuse for not serving a delicious fresh salad.

4 green onions
½ cucumber
3 carrots
6 large tomatoes
10 button mushrooms
3 stems celery
1 green pepper, seeded and chopped
15-20 tiny cauliflower flowerets
15-20 radishes, quartered
1 tbsp chopped watercress, or mustard and cress
2 sprigs fresh green coriander leaf, or chopped parsley
¾ tsp salt
¾ tsp freshly ground black pepper
2½ tbsps cider vinegar
1¼ tbsps lemon juice
5 tbsps olive or vegetable oil
Pinch mustard powder
Liquid sweetener to taste
8 lettuce leaves for garnish

Step 3 Cut the carrot into thin pieces, slicing diagonally with a sharp knife.

Step 9 Whisk all the dressing ingredients together using a fork or eggbeater whisk, until the mixture becomes thick and cloudy.

1. Trim the green onions and slice them diagonally into thin slices.

2. Peel the cucumber and quarter it lengthwise. Use a sharp knife to remove the soft, seedy center, discard this, and dice the remaining flesh.

3. Peel and carrots and slice them thinly, cutting the carrots diagonally with a sharp knife.

4. Cut a small cross into the skins of each tomato, and plunge into boiling water for 30 seconds. Remove the tomatoes and carefully peel away the blanched skin from the fruit. Quarter the peeled tomatoes and cut away the tough green stalk.

5. Thinly slice the mushrooms and sticks of celery.

6. Cut the pepper in half lengthwise and remove all the seeds and the white pith. Discard this, and chop the flesh.

7. Break the cauliflower flowerets into small pieces, and quarter the radishes.

8. Roughly chop the watercress, or mustard and cress, along with the coriander leaves or parsley.

9. For the dressing mix together all the remaining ingredients, except for the lettuce leaves. Whisk thoroughly using a fork, or eggbeater, until the mixture becomes thick and cloudy.

10. Arrange the lettuce leaves on a serving dish, and pile the prepared vegetables on top.

11. Just before serving, spoon a little of the dressing over the salad and serve the remainder separately in a small jug.

Cook's Notes

Time
Preparation takes about 20 minutes.

Variation
Use any combination of your own favorite vegetables in this recipe.

Serving Idea
Serve with cheese or chicken for a light lunch.

SERVES 4

87 kilocalories per serving

BLACK OLIVE AND CAULIFLOWER SALAD

The exciting flavors of the Mediterranean combine in this recipe to produce a refreshingly different salad.

⅔ cup black olives
1 large cauliflower
1 large Spanish onion
5 tbsps olive oil
⅔ cup water
Juice ½ lemon
3½ tbsps tomato paste
Salt and freshly ground black pepper
2½ tbsps fresh chopped parsley

Step 1 To loosen the stones before pitting, roll the olives firmly on a flat surface using the palm of your hand.

1. Roll the olives firmly on a flat surface with the palm of your hands to loosen the stones. Remove the stones using a cherry pitter or the tip of a potato peeler. Chop the olives roughly and set aside.

2. Trim the leaves from the cauliflower and break it into small flowerets.

3. Peel the onion and slice it into rings.

4. Heat the oil in a large sauté pan and gently cook the cauliflower for 2 minutes. Remove the cauliflower to a plate, and cook the onion in the same pan, in the same way.

5. Return the cauliflower to the pan and add the water and the lemon juice. Bring to the boil, reduce the heat and simmer until tender, adding a little more water should the mixture begin to boil dry.

6. Using a slotted spoon, remove the cauliflower from the sauté pan, reserving the juices.

Step 3 Slice the onion into rings by piercing the peeled vegetable with a fork to hold it steady whilst you slice.

7. Add the tomato paste to the liquid and boil rapidly to reduce.

8. Stir the olives into the pan and heat through.

9. Arrange the cauliflower flowerets on a serving dish, and spoon the olive sauce over the top. Chill well.

10. Sprinkle with the chopped parsley just before serving.

Cook's Notes

Time
Preparation takes about 20 minutes, cooking takes approximately 20 minutes, plus chiling time.

Cook's Tip
Add a bay leaf to the cauliflower during the cooking to reduce the strong smell.

Variation
Use green olives instead of black.

SERVES 4

99 kilocalories per serving

STIR-FRIED SALAD

Stir fries are served hot, but the ingredients are cooked so quickly that they retain all of their crunchiness.

1 onion
2 large leeks
5 tbsps olive oil
2 cloves garlic, minced
½lb snow peas, topped and tailed
¼lb bean sprouts, or lentil sprouts
Salt and freshly ground black pepper
1 tbsp fresh chopped coriander leaf

1. Peel the onion and cut it into thin rings.

Step 1 Pierce the onion with a fork to hold it steady whilst you slice it into thin rings.

2. Trim the leeks and cut down the length of one side. Open the leek out and wash it thoroughly under running water.

3. Cut the leek into three pieces, then thinly slice each piece lengthwise into thin strips.

4. Heat the oil in a large wok or frying pan, and add the onions and garlic. Cook for 2 minutes, stirring all the time until the onions have softened but not browned.

5. Add the snow peas and sliced leeks to the wok and continue stir-frying for 4 minutes.

6. Add the remaining ingredients and cook briskly for a further 2 minutes. Serve piping hot.

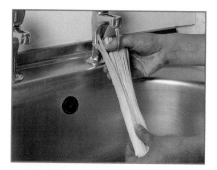

Step 2 Rinse the split leek under running water, separating the leaves to wash out any grit or dirt.

Step 3 Cut the pieces of leek lengthwise into thin strips.

 Cook's Notes

 Time
Preparation takes 15 minutes, cooking takes approximately 10 minutes.

Cook's Tip
Sprout your own beans or lentils by putting them into a glass jar, rinse thoroughly and pour in fresh water each day, cover with muslin, and stand the jar on a sunny windowsill. After 3-4 days, the beans or lentils will have sprouted.

 Serving Idea
Serve this dish with rice, and sprinkle it liberally with soy sauce.

SERVES 6
84 kilocalories per serving

RATATOUILLE

This delicious vegetable casserole from the south of France has become a great favorite the world over.

2 eggplants
Salt
4 zucchini
5 tbsps olive oil
2 Spanish onions
2 green or red peppers
2½ tsps chopped fresh basil
1 large clove garlic, minced
2 x 1lb 12 oz cans of peeled plum tomatoes
Salt and freshly ground black pepper
⅔ cup dry white wine

1. Cut the eggplants in half lengthwise and score each cut surface diagonally, using the point of a sharp knife.

2. Sprinkle the eggplants liberally with salt and allow to stand for 30 minutes to degorge. After this time, rinse them thoroughly and pat them dry.

3. Roughly chop the eggplants and slice the zucchini thickly. Set them to one side.

4. Peel the onions and half them. Cut them into thin slices with a sharp knife.

5. Cut the peppers in half lengthwise and remove and discard the seeds and white pith. Chop the flesh roughly.

6. Heat the oil in a large saucepan, and fry the onion slices for 5 minutes until they are soft and just beginning to brown.

7. Stir in the peppers and zucchini, and cook gently for 5 minutes until they begin to soften. Remove all the vegetables from the pan and set them aside.

8. Put the chopped eggplants into the saucepan with the

Step 5 Remove and discard the seeds and white pith from the halved peppers.

Step 8 Gently fry the chopped eggplant in the vegetable juices and oil, until they begin to brown.

vegetable juices. Cook gently until it begins to brown, then add all the other ingredients to the pan.

9. Add the cans of tomatoes, the garlic and the basil to the saucepan along with the sautéed vegetables, mixing well to blend in evenly. Bring to the boil, then reduce the heat and simmer for 15 minutes, or until the liquid in the pan has been reduced and is thick.

10. Add the wine to the pan and continue cooking for a further 15 minutes, before serving straight away, or chiling and serving cold.

Cook's Notes

Time
Preparation takes 20 minutes, plus 30 minutes standing time. Cooking takes approximately 35 minutes.

Preparation
Make sure that the degorged eggplant is rinsed thoroughly to remove any saltiness, otherwise this will spoil the flavor of the finished dish.

Cook's Tip
If the liquid in the pan is still thin and excessive after the full cooking time, remove the vegetables and boil the juices rapidly until they have reduced and thickened.

SERVES 4

239 kilocalories per serving

LIME ROASTED CHICKEN

This simply made, but unusual, main course is very low in calories and high in tangy flavor.

---

4 chicken breast portions, each weighing about 8oz
Salt and freshly ground black pepper
4 limes
2½ tsps white wine vinegar
6 tbsps olive oil
2½ tsps fresh chopped basil

---

1. Rub the chicken portions all over with salt and black pepper. Place in a shallow ovenproof dish, and set aside.

2. Carefully pare away thin strips of the rind only from 2 of the limes, using a lemon parrer. Cut these 2 limes in half and squeeze the juice.

3. Add the lime juice to the vinegar and 4 tbsps of the olive oil in a small dish, along with the strips of rind, and mix well.

4. Pour the oil and lime juice mixture over the chicken por-

tions in the dish. Cover and refrigerate for about 4 hours or overnight.

5. Remove the covering from the dish in which the chicken is marinating, and baste the chicken well with the marinade mixture. Place into a preheated oven 375°F and cook for 30-35 minutes, or until the chicken is well roasted and tender.

6. In the meantime, peel away the rind and white pith from the remaining 2 limes. Cut the limes into thin slices using a sharp knife.

7. Heat the remaining oil in a small frying pan and add the lime slices and basil. Cook quickly for 1 minute, or until the fragrance rises up from the basil and the limes just begin to soften.

8. Serve the chicken portions on a serving platter, garnished with the fried lime slices and a little extra fresh basil, if desired.

Step 5 After marinating for 4 hours, the chicken portions will look slightly cooked and the meat will have turned a pale opaque color.

Step 7 Fry the lime slices very quickly in the hot oil until they just begin to soften.

Cook's Notes

 Time
Preparation takes 25 minutes, plus 4 hours marinating time. Cooking takes 40 minutes.

 **Preparation**
The chicken can be prepared in advance and marinated overnight.

 Variation
Use lemons instead of limes, and thyme instead of basil.

 Watchpoint
Puncture the chicken with a skewer at its thickest point and when the resulting juices run clear, it is ready.

SERVES 4

300 kilocalories per serving

CHICKEN ESCALOPES

Chicken is an excellent meat to eat when on a low calorie diet, as it is extremely low in fat. There are a multitude of different methods of cooking chicken, and this one although one of the simplest, is also one of the most delicious.

---

4 chicken breasts, boned and skinned
1 egg white
10 tbsps whole-wheat breadcrumbs
1¼ tbsps chopped fresh sage
Salt and freshly ground black pepper
2½ tbsps walnut oil
½ cup low calorie mayonnaise
⅔ cup natural unset yogurt
1¼ tsps grated fresh horseradish
2½ tbsps chopped walnuts
Lemon slices and chopped walnuts to garnish

---

1. Pat the chicken breasts dry with paper towels.

2. Whisk the egg whites with a fork until they just begin to froth, but are still liquid.

3. Carefully brush all surfaces of the chicken breasts with the beaten egg white.

4. Put the breadcrumbs onto a shallow plate and mix in the chopped sage. Season with a little salt and freshly ground black pepper.

5. Place the chicken breasts, one at a time, onto the plate of breadcrumbs and sage, and carefully press this mixture onto the surfaces of the chicken.

6. Put the oil into a large shallow pan, and gently fry the prepared chicken breasts on each side for 5 minutes until they are lightly golden and tender. Set them aside, and keep warm.

7. Mix all the remaining ingredients except for the garnish, in a small bowl, whisking well to blend the yogurt and mayonnaise evenly.

8. Place the cooked chicken breasts on a serving dish, and spoon a little of the sauce over. Serve garnished with the lemon slices and additional chopped nuts.

Step 2 Whisk the egg white with a fork until it becomes frothy, but still liquid.

Step 5 Press the breadcrumb and sage mixture onto all surfaces of the chicken breasts, making sure that they are covered evenly.

Cook's Notes

Time
Preparation takes about 20 minutes, cooking takes 10-15 minutes.

Variation
Use almonds instead of walnuts in this recipe, and limes instead of lemons. Oranges and hazelnuts make another delicious variation.

Serving Idea
Serve with lightly cooked green beans and new potatoes, or rice.

SERVES 4

230 kilocalories per serving

PAPRIKA SCHNITZEL

Thin slices of pork tenderloin are served with a rich tasting paprika sauce for a delicious low calorie meal.

8 thin slices pork tenderloin cut along the fillet
Salt and freshly ground black pepper
1 clove garlic, minced
3¾ tbsps vegetable oil
1 medium-sized onion
1 red pepper
1 green pepper
1¼ tbsps paprika
⅔ cup beef stock
½ cup red wine
3¾ tbsps tomato paste
⅔ cup natural low fat yogurt

Step 1 Flatten the pork slices out with a rolling pin until they are ¼-inch thick.

1. Trim the slices of pork to remove any fat, and flatten them out with a rolling pin until they are ¼-inch thick.

2. Rub both sides of the pork slices with salt, pepper, and garlic, then allow to stand in a refrigerator for 30 minutes.

3. Heat the oil in a large frying pan, and cook the pork slices in several batches if necessary, until they are well browned and cooked right through. This will take approximately 4 minutes on each side.

4. Remove the pork from the pan, set aside, and keep warm.

5. Peel the onion and thinly slice it into rings, steadying it with a fork as you cut. Cut the peppers in half and remove and discard the seeds and white pith. Slice the peppers lengthwise into thin strips.

6. Add the onion rings and the sliced peppers to the oil and meat juices in the frying pan, and cook quickly for about 3-4 minutes until they are soft but not browned.

7. Add the paprika, stock, wine and tomato paste to the frying pan with the vegetables, and bring the mixture to the boil.

8. Reduce the heat and simmer until the liquid has evapo-

Step 6 Fry the onions and peppers together for 3-4 minutes until they have softened but not browned.

rated and the sauce has thickened. Season with salt and pepper to taste.

9. Arrange the pork slices on a serving dish, and pour the paprika sauce over the top of them.

10. Beat the yogurt in a bowl until it is smooth.

11. Carefully drizzle the yogurt over the paprika sauce to make an attractive pattern. Swirl it gently into the sauce to blend, but take care not to incorporate it completely. Serve hot.

Cook's Notes

 Time
Preparation takes 30 minutes, cooking takes approximately 20 minutes.

 Freezing
This dish freezes well.

Preparation
This dish may be made in advance, covered with foil, then reheated in a moderate oven when required.

Cook's Tip
If the yogurt is too thick to drizzle properly, whisk in a little water or skim milk to thin it to the required consistency.

SERVES 4
198 kilocalories per serving

CHICKEN WITH BLACKCURRANT SAUCE

The sharp tang of blackcurrants makes an ideal partner for lightly cooked chicken.

4 chicken breasts, boned and skinned
4 tbsps sesame oil
1⅓ cups fresh blackcurrants
Juice of 1 orange
⅔ cup red wine
Artificial sweetener to taste
Orange slices and fresh blackcurrants to garnish

1. Season the chicken breasts with a little salt. Heat the oil in a shallow frying pan.

Step 2 Gently fry the chicken breasts in the hot oil until they are golden brown on all sides.

2. Gently fry the chicken breasts for 4-5 minutes on each side, until they are golden brown and tender.

3. Top and tail the blackcurrants and put them into a small pan, along with the orange juice and red wine. Bring to the boil, then cover and simmer gently until the blackcurrants are soft.

4. Using a liquidizer or food processor, blend the black-currants and the cooking juice for 30 seconds.

Step 5 Press the blackcurrant purée through a metal sieve with a wooden spoon, to remove all the pips and skins.

Step 6 Simmer the sieved fruit purée until it has thickened and the liquid has reduced.

5. Rub the blended purée through a nylon sieve with the back of a spoon, pressing the fruit through to reserve all the juice and pulp but leaving the pips in the sieve.

6. Put the sieved purée into a small saucepan and heat gently, stirring constantly until the liquid has reduced and the sauce is thick and smooth.

7. Arrange the chicken breasts on a serving dish, and spoon the blackcurrant sauce over. Garnish with orange slices and fresh blackcurrants.

Cook's Notes

Time
Preparation takes 15 minutes, cooking takes approximately 15 minutes.

Preparation
To test if the chicken breasts are cooked, insert a skewer into the thickest part, then press gently, if the juices run clear, the meat is cooked.

Variation
Use blackberries instead of blackcurrants in this recipe.

Serving Idea
Serve with a selection of fresh green vegetables.

SERVES 4
220 kilocalories per serving

KIDNEYS WITH MUSTARD SAUCE

Lambs' kidneys have a wonderful delicate flavor, and when served with a delicious mustard sauce, make a quick and very flavorful main course.

5 tbsps vegetable oil
1½lbs lambs' kidneys
1-2 shallots, peeled and finely chopped
1⅓ cups dry white wine
3¾ tbsps Dijon mustard
Salt, pepper and lemon juice to taste
2½ tbsps fresh chopped parsley

1. Cut the kidneys in half lengthwise, and carefully snip out the core and tough tubes.

2. Heat the oil in a large frying pan, and gently sauté the kidneys for about 10 minutes, stirring them frequently until they are light brown on all sides. Remove the kidneys from the pan and keep them warm.

3. Add the shallots to the sauté pan and cook for about 1 minute, stirring frequently until they soften, but do not brown.

4. Add the wine and bring to the boil, stirring constantly and scraping the pan to remove any brown juices.

5. Allow the wine to boil rapidly for 3-4 minutes, until it has reduced by about 2/3rds. Remove the pan from the heat.

6. Using an eggbeater or fork, mix the mustard into the reduced wine along with salt, pepper, lemon juice to taste, and half of the fresh chopped parsley.

7. Return the kidneys to the pan and cook over a low heat for 1-2 minutes, stirring all the time to heat the kidneys through evenly. Serve immediately, sprinkled with the remaining parsley.

Step 1 Trim any fat or tubes away from the core of each kidney, using a sharp knife or small pair of scissors.

Step 2 Sauté the kidneys in the hot oil, stirring them frequently to brown evenly on all sides.

Step 6 Using an eggbeater or fork, blend the mustard into the reduced wine, whisking well to keep the sauce smooth.

Cook's Notes

Time
Preparation takes about 25 minutes, cooking takes 15 minutes.

Variation
Use chicken livers in place of the lambs' kidney in this recipe.

Watchpoint
Take care not to cook the kidneys for too long as they will toughen if overcooked.

SERVES 4

254 kilocalories per serving

SOLE KEBABS

Fish is highly nutritious, economical to prepare, and makes an ideal contribution to a healthy diet.

8 fillets of sole
5 tbsps olive oil
1 clove garlic, minced
Juice ½ lemon
Finely grated rind ½ lemon
Salt and freshly ground black pepper
3 drops of Tabasco, or pepper sauce
3 medium-sized zucchini
1 medium-sized green pepper
Freshly chopped parsley for garnish

1. Using a sharp knife, carefully peel the skin from the backs of each sole fillet.

Step 1 Use a sharp knife to carefully cut between the meat of the fish and the skin. Lift the meat up and away as you cut, keeping the blade of the knife away from you.

Step 2 Cut the sole fillets in half lengthwise, and roll the slices up jelly roll fashion.

2. Cut each sole fillet in half lengthwise, and roll each slice up jelly roll fashion.

3. Mix together the oil, garlic, lemon juice, rind, and seasonings in a small bowl.

4. Put the rolls of fish into a shallow dish and pour over the lemon and oil marinade. Cover the dish and allow to stand in a cool place for at least 2 hours.

5. Cut the zucchini into ¼-inch slices.

6. Cut the peppers in half lengthwise and remove the white core and the seeds. Chop the pepper flesh into 1-inch squares.

7. Carefully thread the marinated sole fillets onto kebab skewers, alternating these with pieces of the prepared vegetables. Brush each kebab with a little of the oil and lemon marinade.

8. Arrange the kebabs on a broiler pan and cook under a moderately hot broiler for about 8 minutes, turning frequently to prevent them from burning, and brushing with the extra marinade to keep them moist.

9. Arrange the kebabs on a serving dish, and sprinkle with the chopped parsley for garnish.

Step 7 Thread the marinated rolls of fish onto kebab skewers, alternating these with vegetables for color.

Cook's Notes

Time
Preparation takes about 30 minutes, plus marinating time. Cooking takes approximately 8 minutes.

Preparation
After 2 hours marinating, the sole will look opaque and have a partially cooked appearance.

Cook's Tip
These kebabs are ideal for cooking out of doors on a barbeque.

SERVES 6
275 kilocalories per serving

CASSEROLE OF VEAL AND MUSHROOMS

Veal is a low fat meat and is delicious when served in this tomato and mushroom sauce.

3lbs lean pie veal
Salt and freshly ground black pepper
5 tbsps olive oil
2 shallots, finely chopped
½ clove garlic, minced
½ cup dry white wine
1⅓ cups strong brown stock
1 cup canned tomatoes, drained and chopped
1 bouquet garni
2 strips lemon peel
1 cup small button mushrooms
2½ tbsps fresh chopped parsley

1. Dice the meat into bite-sized pieces, using a sharp knife.

2. Sprinkle the pieces of meat with salt and pepper, then allow to stand for about 30 minutes.

3. Heat half of the oil in a large frying pan, and cook the pieces of meat for 5-10 minutes, stirring them frequently until they are browned on all sides. Remove the meat from the pan and set it aside.

4. Add the shallots and garlic to the oil and meat juices in the pan, lower the heat and cook until softened, but not colored. Return the veal to the pan and mix well.

5. Add the wine, stock, tomatoes, bouquet garni and lemon peel to the meat mixture, and bring to the boil.

6. Transfer the veal to an ovenproof casserole. Cover with a tight-fitting lid and bake in a pre-heated oven 325°F for

Step 3 Gently brown the veal in the hot oil, stirring it frequently until it has browned on all sides.

Step 4 Cook the garlic and shallots in the hot oil and meat juices gently, taking care to soften, but not brown them.

about 1¼ hours, or until the meat is tender.

7. Heat the remaining oil in a clean frying pan, and gently stir in the mushrooms, cooking them for 2-3 minutes until they begin to soften, but are not properly cooked.

8. After the casserole cooking time has finished, stir in the partially cooked mushrooms and continue cooking in the oven for a further 15 minutes.

9. Sprinkle with the chopped parsley before serving.

Cook's Notes

 Time
Preparation takes about 30 minutes, cooking takes approximately 1½ hours.

 **Variation**
Use lamb, or beef, instead of the veal in this recipe.

 Serving Idea
Serve with new potatoes, pasta, or rice.

 Watchpoint
Do not allow the garlic and onions to brown, or it will impair the flavor of the veal.

SERVES 4
157 kilocalories per serving

EGGPLANT AND CHICKEN CHILI

This unusual dish is both delicious and filling.

2 medium-sized eggplants
5 tbsps sesame oil
2 cloves garlic, minced
4 green onions
1 green chili, finely chopped
¾lb boned and skinned chicken breast
5 tbsps light soy sauce
2½ tbsps stock, or water
1¼ tbsps tomato paste
1 tsp cornstarch
Liquid sweetener to taste

1. Cut the eggplant into quarters lengthwise, using a sharp knife. Slice the eggplant quarters into pieces approximately ½-inch thick.

2. Put the eggplant slices into a bowl and sprinkle liberally with salt. Stir well to coat evenly. Cover with plastic wrap and leave to stand for 30 minutes.

3. Rinse the eggplant slices very thoroughly under running water, then pat dry with a clean tea cloth.

4. Heat half of the oil in a wok, or large frying pan, and gently cook the garlic until it is soft, but not colored.

5. Add the eggplant slices to the wok and cook, stirring frequently, for 3-4 minutes.

6. Using a sharp knife, slice the green onions into thin di-

Step 6 Cut the green onions diagonally into small pieces, approximately ½ inch long.

agonal strips. Stir the green onions together with the chili into the cooked eggplant, and cook for a further 1 minute. Remove the eggplant and onion from the pan, and set aside, keeping warm.

7. Cut the chicken breast into thin slices with a sharp knife.

8. Heat the remaining oil in the wok, and fry the chicken pieces for approximately 2 minutes or until they have turned white and are cooked thoroughly.

9. Return the eggplant and onions to the pan and cook, stirring continuously, for 2 minutes or until heated through completely.

10. Mix together the remaining ingredients and pour these over the chicken and eggplants in the wok, stirring constantly until the sauce has thickened and cleared. Serve immediately.

Cook's Notes

Time
Preparation takes about 10 minutes, cooking takes approximately 15 minutes.

Cook's Tip
The vegetables can be prepared well in advance, but the eggplants should be removed from the salt after 30 minutes, or they will become too dehydrated.

Variation
Use turkey instead of chicken in this recipe, and zucchini in place of the eggplants.

Serving Idea
Serve this recipe as part of a more extensive Chinese style meal.

SERVES 4
170 kilocalories per serving
FRUIT PLATE

This medley of fruit can be varied to suit your taste and is served without a syrupy liquid, so is low in calories.

1 green fig
2 kiwi fruit
2 fresh dates
1 guava
1 paw paw
¾ cup lychees
½ small pineapple
1 fresh mango
¾ cup seedless grapes
½ small melon
½ lb watermelon
2½ tbsps orange juice
2½ tbsps lemon juice
½ cup chopped walnuts, or pine kernels (optional)

1. Select a large, shallow serving platter on which to arrange the fruit.

2. Cut the figs into quarters lengthwise and arrange on a plate.

3. Peel the kiwi fruits, and remove any hard core from the stem end. Slice the fruit thinly and arrange alongside the figs, reserving a few slices for the watermelon.

4. Cut the dates in half lengthwise and remove the stones. Place the dates on the serving plate.

5. Cut the guavas in half and slice these into wedges with a sharp knife. Peel the paw paw and slice this into thin crescents. Arrange the guava slices and paw paw alternately onto the plate along with the other prepared fruit.

6. Peel the lychees and remove the stones from the stalk end, using the rounded tip of a swivel potato peeler. Discard the stones, and place the fruit on the serving platter.

7. Peel the pineapple and cut away any brown eyes which may remain in the flesh. Cut the pineapple into slices and remove the core, using a sharp knife or apple corer. Cut the pineapple slices into small wedges and arrange on the plate.

8. Peel the mango and cut the flesh into slices, discarding the stone.

9. Halve the seedless grapes. Place the mango and grapes in an alternate pattern, alongside the rest of the fruit on the serving plate.

10. Peel the melon, cut into half, and remove the seeds. Slice the melon flesh into small wedges.

11. Leave the peel and pips in the watermelon, and cut this into small wedges, approximately the same size as the previous melon. Arrange the melon wedges on either side of the plate and decorate with the remaining kiwi fruit if used.

12. Mix together the lemon, juice, orange juice and chopped nuts, and sprinkle this dressing evenly over the fruit on the plate. Cover with plastic wrap and chill well before serving.

Step 6 Remove the stones from the lychees by scooping them out from the stalk end with the rounded end of a potato peeler.

Cook's Notes

Time
Preparation takes about 30 minutes, plus chiling time.

Preparation
Canned lychees could be used in place of the fresh fruit in this recipe, as could canned pineapples, kiwis and mangoes, but make sure they are packed in natural juice which should be drained before serving.

Variation
Use any selection of your favorite fruits in this recipe.

SERVES 4

63 kilocalories per serving

STRAWBERRY YOGURT ICE

Ice cream is usually forbidden on a low calorie diet, but when prepared with low fat natural yogurt and fresh fruit, it can provide a welcome treat.

1⅔ cups fresh strawberries
1⅓ cups low fat natural yogurt
2½ tsps gelatin
2½ tbsps boiling water
1 egg white
Liquid sweetener to taste
Few fresh strawberries for decoration

1. Remove and discard the green stalks and leaves from the top of the strawberries. Roughly chop the fruit.

2. Place the strawberries into a liquidizer, or food processor, along with the yogurt. Blend until smooth.

3. Sprinkle the gelatin over the boiling water in a small bowl. Stand the bowl into another, and pour in enough boiling water to come halfway up the sides of the dish.

4. Allow the gelatin to stand, without stirring, until it has dissolved and the liquid has cleared.

5. Pour the strawberry mixture into a bowl, and stir in the dissolved gelatin, mixing well to blend evenly. Place the bowl into a deep freeze and chill until just icy around the edges.

6. Remove the bowl from the deep freeze and beat until the chilled mixture is smooth. Return the bowl to the deep freeze and freeze once again in the same way.

7. Remove the bowl from the deep freeze a second time, and whisk with an electric mixer until smooth. Whisk the egg white until it forms soft peaks.

8. Fold the whisked egg white into the partially set straw-

Step 2 Blend the strawberries and yogurt together in a liquidizer or food processor, until they are smooth.

Step 5 Remove the strawberry mixture from the freezer when it is just beginning to set and has frozen around the edges.

berry mixture, carefully lifting and cutting the mixture to keep it light.

9. Sweeten with liquid sweetener to taste, then pour the strawberry ice into a shallow sided ice cream dish, and return to the freezer to freeze until completely set.

10. Remove the ice cream 10 minutes before serving to soften slightly. Pile into serving dishes and decorate with a few extra strawberries.

Cook's Notes

Time
Preparation takes about 15 minutes, plus freezing time.

Cook's Tip
Use frozen or canned strawberries in place of the fresh strawberries, but drain all the juice away first.

Variation
Use any other soft fruit in place of the strawberries. It may be preferable to sieve blackcurrants or raspberries to remove the pips, before adding to the yogurt as a purée.

SERVES 4
109 kilocalories per serving
BLACKBERRY FLUFF

Fresh blackberries have a delicious flavor, especially the wild ones picked from hedgerows.

1lb fresh blackberries
1⅓ cups natural low fat set yogurt
2 egg whites
Liquid sweetener to taste
Pieces of angelica and whole blackberries to decorate

---

1. Wash the blackberries thoroughly and place them in a saucepan with no extra water, other than that which is left on their surfaces after washing. Cover the pan with a tight fitting lid, and cook over a low heat for 5-10 minutes, stirring occasionally until the fruit has softened. Cool slightly.

2. Press the cooked blackberries through a nylon sieve, using the back of a spoon to press out the juice and pulp. Discard the pips and reserve the purée.

3. Put the yogurt into a large bowl and beat in the blackberry purée until it is smooth.

Step 2 Press the cooked blackberries through a metal sieve, using the back of a wooden spoon to push through the juice and pulp, leaving the pips in the sieve.

4. Whisk the egg whites until they form very stiff peaks.

5. Fold these into the blackberry purée, trying not to over mix the ingredients, so as to create an attractive marbled effect.

6. Sweeten with the liquid sweetener to taste, then pile into serving dishes and decorate with the whole blackberries and angelica pieces. Chill before serving.

Step 4 Whisk the egg whites until they form very stiff peaks.

Step 5 Lightly fold the egg whites into the blackberry mixture, to create an attractive marbled effect.

Cook's Notes

Time
Preparation takes about 20 minutes. Cooking time takes approximately 10 minutes, plus chiling time.

Preparation
This recipe can also be partially frozen to create a cooling summer dessert.

Variation
Use raspberries, or strawberries, in place of blackberries in this recipe.

SERVES 4
101 kilocalories per serving

SUNBURST FIGS

Fresh figs can make a most attractive dessert and have the added benefit of being very low in calories.

---

4 fresh figs
⅔ cup redcurrants in small bunches
6 oranges
1¼ tsps orange flower water

---

1. Trim the stalks away from the top of the figs, but do not peel them.

2. Cut the figs into quarters lengthwise, taking care not to sever them completely at the base.

Step 2 Cut the figs into quarters lengthwise with a sharp knife, taking great care not to sever the fruit completely through the base.

3. Press the fig quarters open gently with your fingers, to make a flower shape. Place each fig carefully on a serving plate.

4. Arrange the small bunches of redcurrants carefully on the center of each fig.

5. Cut 2 of the oranges in half, and squeeze out the juice. Mix this juice with the orange flower water in a small jug.

6. Carefully cut away the peel and white pith from the re-

Step 3 Carefully press open the quarters of each fig to make an attractive flower shape.

Step 7 Cut the orange segments away from the peeled fruit with a sharp knife, slicing carefully between the flesh and the thin membranes inside each segment.

maining 4 oranges.

7. Using a sharp knife, cut the segments of orange away from the inside of the thin membranes, keeping each piece intact as a crescent shape.

8. Arrange the orange segments in between the petals of the fig flower on the serving plate.

9. Spoon equal amounts of the orange sauce over each fig, and chill thoroughly before serving.

Cook's Notes

Time
Preparation takes about 15 minutes, plus chiling time.

Variation
Use ruby grapefruit segments and blackcurrants in place of the oranges and redcurrants in this recipe.

Serving Idea
Freeze the currants before placing them on the figs, to give an attractive finish to this dessert.

SERVES 4

125 kilocalories per serving

MANGO SORBET

This delicious cool sorbet can be used either as a dessert, or as a refresher between courses on a low calorie meal.

3 mangoes
Juice ½ lime
½ cup dry white wine
½ cup mineral water
1 egg white
Liquid sweetener to taste (optional)

1. Peel the mango and cut away the flesh from around the large center stone.

2. Put the mango flesh into a liquidizer or food processor, and blend until smooth.

3. In a bowl, mix together the lime juice, wine and mineral water.

4. Place the mango purée in a freezer and freeze until just beginning to set around the edges.

5. Break up the ice crystals in the mango mixture using a fork.

6. Whisk the egg white until it is stiff, then fold this carefully and thoroughly into the mango mixture. Sweeten with liquid sweetener to taste, if used.

7. Return the mango mixture to the deep freeze, and freeze until completely set.

8. To serve, remove from the deep freeze 10 minutes before required, then spoon into individual serving dishes.

Step 2 Purée the mango flesh in a liquidizer or food processor, until it is smooth.

Step 5 Break up the ice crystals which have formed in the mango mixture into small pieces using the back of a fork.

Cook's Notes

 Time
Preparation takes about 15 minutes, plus freezing time.

 Variation
Use any other favorite fruit in place of the mango.

 Serving Idea
Serve with fresh fruit.

SUGAR
FREE

Introduction

In today's health-conscious atmosphere we are all becoming more aware of the disadvantages of a high sugar intake – increasing levels of obesity and tooth decay are the most obvious results of just such a diet. We now eat as much sugar in two weeks as people of two centuries ago did in one year, yet as we live less active lives, we actually require less energy than our forefathers.

There are many misconceptions about the properties of sugar. Contrary to what many people believe, sugar does not contain any nutrients and all types of sugar, whether white or brown, or in the form of honey or maple syrup, have the same calorific value. Sugar, or sucrose to give it its technical name, is a complex carbohydrate made up of two simple sugars. The first, fructose, is the sweetest and is found naturally in fruits. The second, glucose, is formed by the body during the digestion of plants and vegetables. Sugars are all digested in the same way: the sugar is broken down into glucose, which then travels around in the blood as energy; if this energy isn't used, it is stored as fat reserves.

By eating naturally sweet foods we can educate our palates to prefer these to over-sweet, sugared foods. The extra chewing needed will also produce more saliva to clean away the sugary film from the teeth and help prevent decay. As naturally sweet foods also take longer to digest, our bodies will not experience the short-lived artificial "highs" that refined sugars produce.

Unfortunately, it is not always possible to leave sugar out of recipes as it can be vital for a dish's preservation or structure. However, cutting down our sugar intake gradually and avoiding those processed foods which contain sugar is a big step towards a more healthful diet. In addition, eating more naturally sweet foods containing fructose, such as strawberries, not only reduces calorie intake but also provides some nutritional benefits from the food, including vitamins and fiber.

Switching to a healthful diet does not mean sacrificing taste but rather replacing refined sugars with more natural sugars and sweet fruits. The recipes in this book do just that, providing a varied selection of wholesome dishes that are delicious too!

SERVES 6-8

GOLDEN RAISIN SODA BREAD

Golden raisins add a natural sweetness which makes this bread ideal for serving as a tea-time treat.

1lb all-purpose white flour
1¼ tsps salt
1¼ tsps baking soda
1¼ tsps cream of tartar
1⅓ cups sour milk
⅔ cup golden raisins

1. Sift together the flour, salt, baking soda and cream of tartar in a mixing bowl.

2. Add the golden raisins and mix into the flour quickly, making a slight well in the center of the flour as you do so.

3. Pour the milk into the well in the flour, and mix with a round bladed knife to form a firm, but not too stiff dough.

4. Turn the dough onto a lightly floured board, and knead quickly to bring all the ingredients together well.

5. Shape the dough into a round, and flatten it slightly with the palm of your hand.

6. Place the dough round on a lightly greased and floured cookie sheet. Cut a deep cross into the top of the dough with a sharp knife.

7. Bake the dough in a preheated oven 400°F for 25 minutes.

8. After this time, turn the loaf upside down on the cookie sheet and return to the oven for a further 10 minutes to dry out completely.

9. Wrap the baked loaf in a damp cloth, and place on a wire rack to cool completely.

Step 6 Cut a deep cross into the top of the bread dough using a sharp knife.

Step 8 Turn the loaf upside down on the cookie sheet before returning to the oven for a further 10 minutes.

 Cook's Notes

 Time
Preparation takes 15 minutes, cooking takes 35 minutes.

Variation
Use whole-wheat flour instead of the white flour in this recipe.

Preparation
To test that the loaf is completely cooked, tap the base with your fingers and if it sounds hollow it is ready.

 Cook's Tip
If you do not have sour milk, use fresh milk with 1 tbsp of natural yogurt added.

 Freezing
This bread freezes well.

MAKES 10-12

RICH FRUIT BISCUITS

Fruit biscuits are always a firm favorite and do not need any added sugar when made with plenty of fruit.

½lb all-purpose flour
1¼ tsps cream of tartar
¾ tsp baking soda
⅓ tsp salt
3 tbsps butter
½ cup golden raisins
¾ tbsp sunflower seeds
½oz fresh stem ginger
2 eggs
Extra milk for blending
Beaten egg, for glaze

Step 9 Roll out the dough to no less than ½-inch thick.

Step 2 Rub the butter into the sieved flour until the mixture resembles fine breadcrumbs.

1. Mix the flour, cream of tartar, baking soda and salt together, and sieve it twice through a metal sieve to aerate completely.

2. Put the sieved flour into a large bowl, and rub in the butter until the mixture resembles fine breadcrumbs.

3. Stir the golden raisins and the sunflower seeds into the flour and butter mixture.

4. Peel the ginger, and cut or grate it into very small pieces.

5. Using a pestle and mortar or the handle of a large knife, crush the ginger until it becomes a paste.

6. Put the ginger into a small bowl along with the eggs, and beat together with a fork until they are evenly blended.

7. Add the beaten eggs and ginger to the flour and raisin mixture, mixing well to form a soft dough, and adding a little extra milk if the dough is too stiff.

8. Lightly flour a work surface. Turn out the dough and knead it lightly until it becomes smooth.

9. Roll the dough out to approximately ½-inch thick.

10. Cut the dough into 2-inch rounds using a biscuit cutter.

11. Place the biscuits on a greased cookie sheet, and brush each one with the extra beaten egg. Bake in a preheated oven 400°F for 10-15 minutes, or until golden brown and well risen.

Cook's Notes

Time
Preparation takes approximately 15 minutes, cooking takes 10-15 minutes.

Preparation
Do not roll the dough out too thinly, otherwise the biscuits will not rise properly.

Variation
Use other combinations of dried fruit and nuts, or seeds, in place of the golden raisins and sunflower seeds in this recipe.

SERVES 6-8

SUGAR-FREE FRUIT CAKE

There is no need for sugar in a recipe rich in the natural sweetness of dried fruits.

¼lbs all-purpose flour
¾ tsp baking soda
1¼ tsps mixed spice
1¼ tsps ground nutmeg
1 cup butter
2 cups raisins
1⅓ cups currants
2 cups golden raisins
⅔ cup mixed peel
1¼ cups Guinness, or stout
3 eggs

Step 9 The cake batter should drop easily into the prepared pan, but not be too runny, or it will seep around the lining paper.

1. Sift the flour, baking soda, mixed spice and nutmeg into a large bowl, using a metal sieve.

2. Cut the butter into small dice, and rub into the flour using the fingertips, until the mixture resembles fine breadcrumbs.

3. Add all the fruit to the flour and mix well to distribute evenly.

4. Push the flour and fruit mixture away from the center of the bowl to form a slight well.

5. Put the Guinness and the eggs into a large jug and whisk together thoroughly, until frothy.

6. Pour the Guinness and eggs into the well in the center of the flour mixture.

7. Mix the Guinness and eggs together to form a soft batter, using a round bladed knife.

8. Grease and line a 9-inch round cake pan with wax paper.

9. Pour the cake batter into the pan and bake in the center of a preheated oven 325°F for 2 hours. Reduce the temperature to 275°F after the first hour if the cake appears to be cooking too quickly.

10. Test the cake with a skewer to see when it is done. If it is cooked, the skewer will come out clean. Turn the cake onto a wire rack, remove the lining paper and cool it completely before storing in an airtight tin for 2-3 days, before serving.

Cook's Notes

Time
Preparation takes approximately 30 minutes, cooking takes 2 hours.

Variation
Use whole-wheat flour in place of the white flour in this recipe, cider instead of Guinness, and grated apple instead of mixed peel.

Preparation
If the cake is cooking too quickly, the sides will become brown and the center of the cake will rise up into a point. If this should happen, reduce the temperature and cook at a much slower heat. Cover the top of the cake with aluminium foil to prevent it from browning further.

Cook's Tip
The flavor of this cake really does improve if it can be kept in an airtight container for a few days before using.

Freezing
This cake freezes very well for up to 3 months.

SERVES 4-6
GRIDDLE SCONES

The whole fun of these cakes is that they can be eaten directly from the pan in which they are cooked. So gather family and friends around you for a traditional tea-time treat.

1 cup self-rising flour
Pinch salt
3 tbsps butter or margarine
⅔ cup currants
¾ tsp ground nutmeg
1 egg
⅓ cup milk

Step 4 Using a wooden spoon, mix the egg and flour mixture into the flour, stirring from the center of the bowl and drawing the flour in from the sides to form a smooth, thick batter.

Step 1 Rub the butter into the flour with your fingertips, until the mixture resembles fine breadcrumbs.

Step 6 Fry tablespoons of the batter in a hot pan until the undersides have browned lightly and the tops are just set.

1. Mix the flour and salt together, and rub in the butter until the mixture resembles fine breadcrumbs.

2. Stir in the currants and the nutmeg, then push the mixture gently to the sides of the bowl to form a well in the center.

3. Beat together the egg and the milk, and pour the into the well in the center of the flour.

4. Using a wooden spoon, mix the egg and milk mixture into the flour, stirring from the center of the bowl and drawing the flour in from the sides to form a smooth, thick batter.

5. Heat a heavy-based frying pan on top of a moderate heat, and grease with a little butter or oil.

6. Drop tablespoons of the batter into the hot pan, and cook for 2-3 minutes, or until the bases are set and have turned golden brown.

7. Turn the scones over and cook on the other side in the same way.

8. Serve from the pan with sugar-free preserves.

Cook's Notes

Time
Preparation takes 15 minutes, cooking takes about 4 minutes per scone.

Preparation
If the batter is too thick, add a little extra milk until it becomes a soft dropping consistency.

Freezing
These scones freeze well, and can be re-heated by wrapping in a clean dish towel and standing in a warm oven until they are heated through.

SERVES 6-8

FRUIT LOAF

There is no need to add sugar to this recipe as the easy-blend yeast will work on the natural sugars provided by the fruit.

1lb all-purpose flour
¾ tsp cinnamon
¾ tsp nutmeg
¾ tsp salt
1⅓ cups golden raisins
1⅓ cups currants
⅓ cup cut mixed peel
1 package of easy blend yeast
2½ tbsps vegetable oil
1¼ cups lukewarm milk
1 large egg

1. Put the flour, spices and salt into a large mixing bowl.

2. Stir in the golden raisins, currants and mixed peel, mixing well to distribute the fruit evenly.

3. Sprinkle over the yeast, and mix this directly into the dry ingredients.

4. Put the oil, milk and egg into a large jug, and beat together with a fork until the egg is broken up evenly. Add the mixture to the flour, and mix together, stirring until the batter becomes stiff and elastic.

5. Turn the batter onto a lightly floured board, and knead until smooth – approximately 10 minutes.

6. Return the batter to the bowl and cover with a damp cloth or a piece of plastic wrap. Leave the batter in a warm place for about 1 hour to allow the dough to rise.

7. After this time, the dough should be approximately double its original size.

8. Punch the dough down to remove the air, and turn it out once again onto the lightly floured surface.

9. Continue kneading the dough for approximately 5 minutes, then cut in two.

Step 4 Mix the milk mixture into the flour and yeast mixture, stirring until a soft, but elastic, dough is formed.

Step 10 Shape the pieces of dough to fit into 2 lightly greased, or non-stick loaf pans.

10. Shape each piece of dough to fit 2 x 7-inch non-stick loaf pans. Cover each pan lightly with plastic wrap or a damp cloth, and leave once again in a warm place until the loaves have risen to double their size.

11. Bake the loaves for 30-40 minutes in the center of a preheated oven 400°F, removing the loaves from the oven after 20 minutes, and brushing the surfaces with a little milk.

12. To test if the loaves are cooked, turn out of the pans and tap the bases with your knuckles, if it sounds hollow, the loaves are ready.

13. Serve warm, or allow to cool and serve sliced, with butter.

Cook's Notes

Time
Preparation takes approximately 2 hours; cooking takes 40 minutes.

Variation
Use any combination of your favorite dried fruits in this recipe.

Freezing
This recipe freezes well for up to 2 months.

MAKES 10

FRUIT TRUFFLES

These delicious little cakes get all the sweetness they require from fresh bananas.

2 bananas
Juice ½ orange
Finely grated rind 1 orange
1¼ cups ground almonds
¼ cup blanched almonds
1¼ tbsps plain cocoa

1. Chop the bananas into a large bowl and using a potato masher, mash them until they are smooth.

2. Mix in the orange juice and rind.

3. Stir in the ground almonds, mixing well to blend evenly. Place the mixture in a refrigerator and chill for approximately 30 minutes.

4. Using a sharp knife, finely chop the blanched almonds into small pieces.

5. Mix the chopped almonds into the cocoa powder, and placc on a flat plate.

Step 1 Mash the bananas to a smooth pulp using a potato masher.

Step 7 Roll the banana mixture into 10 even-sized balls, using lightly floured hands.

Step 8 Cover each banana truffle with an even coating of chopped nuts and cocoa, pressing this gently onto the surface to ensure it stays in place.

6. Remove the banana mixture from the refrigerator, and divide into 10 portions.

7. Roll each portion into a small ball, using lightly floured hands.

8. Roll each ball into the cocoa and almond mixture, rolling each one evenly to give a good coating. Press gently before placing into a small paper cases, and chilling once again.

Cook's Notes

Time
Preparation takes approximately 25 minutes, plus chilling time.

Cook's Tip
Do not keep these delicious sweets for long after they have been made, or the banana will go brown and wet.

Variation
Use walnuts in place of almonds in this recipe.

MAKES 2lbs

COCONUT RELISH

This unusual relish is a welcome change from the more common fruit relishes.

2 fresh coconuts
½-inch piece fresh root ginger
2 green chilies
1¼ tsps cumin seed
5 tbsps finely chopped fresh coriander leaves
3¾ tbsps lemon juice
¾ tsp salt

1. Crack the coconuts in half, and carefully pour out and reserve the milk.

2. Remove the coconut flesh from inside the shells, and peel off the brown outer skin.

3. Chop the peeled coconut into small pieces.

4. Peel the root ginger and finely chop or grate the flesh.

5. Cut the green chilies in half, remove and discard the seeds, and finely chop the outer flesh.

6. Put the coconut, ginger, chilies, cumin seeds, coriander, lemon and salt into a liquidizer or food processor, and blend with enough coconut milk to produce a thick creamy relish.

7. Pour the mixture into pots and seal well.

8. Keep in a refrigerator and use within 2-3 weeks.

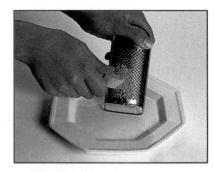

Step 4 Finely chop or grate the peeled root ginger.

Step 2 Peel away the brown skin from the flesh of the coconut using a sharp knife.

Step 6 Blend the relish ingredients with coconut milk in a liquidizer or food processor until it is thick and creamy.

 Cook's Notes

 Time
Preparation takes approximately 20 minutes.

 Freezing
This recipe freezes well.

Preparation
If you do not have a liquidizer or a food processor, the coconut and other ingredients can be grated, but this will not produce such a smooth textured relish.

 Serving Idea
This relish is delicious served with cold meats, curries, or in sandwiches.

MAKES APPROXIMATELY 5lbs

FRUIT CHUTNEY

The use of canned fruit means that this delicious chutney can be prepared at any time of the year.

15oz can pears in natural juice
15oz can peach slices in natural juice
12oz can pineapple chunks in natural juice
8oz can prunes in natural juice
1lb plums
4 cooking apples
½ cup fresh dates, pitted
½ cup ready-to-use dried apricots
1-inch piece fresh root ginger, peeled and thinly sliced
1 cup blanched almonds
1 cup cashew nuts
5 tbsps malt vinegar
¾ tsp ground cloves
1¼ tsps chili powder
2-inch piece cinnamon stick
2 bananas, peeled and sliced

1. Remove the stones from the plums and chop the flesh into fairly large pieces.

2. Drain the fruit juices from the cans of fruit, and set aside. Chop the fruit into large pieces.

3. Cut the apples into four and remove the cores, but do not peel.

4. Finely slice the apple and mix this with the chopped fruit in a large saucepan.

5. Chop the dates and the dried apricots into small pieces. Add the apricots and dates to the saucepan of fruit, along with all the remaining ingredients, except for the reserved juice.

6. Pour over enough of the reserved juice to just cover the fruit.

7. Cover the pan, and bring the chutney to the boil. Reduce the heat and simmer for 15-20 minutes.

8. Remove the lid of the pan and stir the chutney well. Add a little extra juice if required, and continue cooking for a further 10 minutes, uncovered, stirring occasionally to prevent the mixture from burning.

9. When the chutney is thick and most of the liquid has evaporated, divide it between clean warm glass jars. Cover with waxed paper and a tight fitting lid, then store for up to 3 months in a refrigerator.

Step 1 Cut the plums in half and carefully remove the stones. Chop the flesh into fairly large pieces.

Step 9 When cooked, the chutney should be thick and most of the liquid should have evaporated.

Cook's Notes

Time
Preparation takes approximately 15 minutes, cooking takes 30 minutes.

Serving Idea
Serve with cold meats, cheeses, or in sandwiches.

Cook's Tip
Check that the chutney does not stick to the base of the pan, by stirring occasionally whilst it is cooking.

Variation
If you cannot get fresh plums, try using mangoes or apricots.

Freezing
This recipe will freeze well.

MAKES APPROXIMATELY 2lbs

SUGAR-FREE MINCEMEAT

Not only is this recipe free from refined sugar, it is also completely fat free, making it extremely healthful.

3 large red eating apples
1⅓ cups raisins
1⅓ cups currants
1⅓ cups golden raisins
⅔ cup fresh dates
½ cup blanched almonds
⅔ cup brandy or sherry

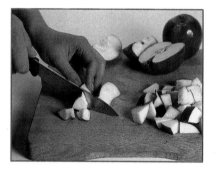

Step 1 Quarter the apples, remove the cores and chop the flesh roughly.

Step 3 Blend the pitted dates with the nuts and brandy, or sherry, until they are fairly coarsely chopped.

Step 4 Mix the date mixture with the apple and fruit mixture, stirring well to blend evenly.

1. Quarter the apples, remove the cores and chop the apple flesh.

2. Put the apples into a liquidizer or food processor, along with the raisins, currants and golden raisins. Chop the fruit finely, then transfer to a large mixing bowl.

3. Carefully remove the stones from the dates and put the fruit into a food processor or liquidizer, along with the nuts and the brandy or sherry. Process until the dates and nuts are roughly chopped.

4. Mix the date mixture into the apple and dried fruit mixture, stirring well to blend all ingredients thoroughly.

5. Divide the mixture between 2-3 clean glass jars, then cover and allow to stand for up to 3 weeks before using.

Cook's Notes

Time
Preparation takes approximately 20 minutes.

Serving Idea
Use in minced pies or apple pie as a natural sweetener.

Freezing
This recipe will freeze, but should be stirred well when thawed to distribute the alcohol evenly.

MAKES 2 cups

CHOCOLATE BUTTER SAUCE

The sugar-free (diabetic) chocolate used in this recipe is readily available in most health food shops.

1 cup water
2 cups sugar-free chocolate, chopped
½ cup butter, cut into small pieces
1¼ tbsps brandy

Step 1 Melt the chocolate in the water over a low heat, stirring until the mixture is smooth.

1. Put the water and the chocolate into a saucepan, and heat over a low heat, stirring until the chocolate has melted.

2. Remove the melted chocolate and water from the heat and slowly stir in the butter, piece by piece, until the mixture becomes thick and glossy.

3. Whisk the brandy into the butter sauce and spoon into an attractive serving dish. This sauce can be served hot or cold.

Step 2 Drop the butter into the melted chocolate, piece by piece, stirring well until it has melted.

Step 3 Beat the brandy into the sauce, whisking until it is thick and glossy.

Cook's Notes

Time
Preparation takes approximately 5 minutes, cooking takes 10 minutes.

Preparation
After melting the chocolate and water together, the mixture should be smooth, with no lumps in it.

Serving Idea
Serve with fresh fruit or pancakes.

Watchpoint
Do not heat the chocolate and water too rapidly or the mixture will curdle.

MAKES 1 cup

MOCHA SAUCE

This unusual coffee chocolate sauce gets its sweetness from the delightfully tangy apricot purée.

1 cup sugar-free chocolate
3¾ tbsps very strong black coffee
½ cup heavy cream
½ cup thick apricot purée (see separate recipe)

Step 3 Stir the heavy cream into the chocolate and coffee mixture, mixing well to blend evenly.

Step 2 Melt the chocolate and coffee together in a bowl which is standing over a saucepan of hot water.

1. Grate the chocolate, or chop it into small pieces with a sharp knife.

2. Put the chocolate and the coffee into a large bowl, and stand the bowl over a saucepan half filled with simmering water. Remove the saucepan and the bowl from the heat, and stir the chocolate gently until it has melted.

3. Add the heavy cream to the melted chocolate, mixing well to blend evenly.

4. Stir in the apricot purée, transfer the chocolate sauce to a serving dish and chill thoroughly.

Cook's Notes

Time
Preparation takes approximately 5 minutes, cooking takes 15 minutes.

Serving Idea
Serve this delicious sauce with fruit or pancakes.

Watchpoint
Take great care not to cook the chocolate and the coffee together too quickly, or the chocolate will separate and curdle.

MAKES APPROXIMATELY 1½ cups

APRICOT PURÉE

This delicious tangy sauce is made with canned apricots in natural juice,
thus making use of the natural sweetness of fruit sugars.

15oz can apricot halves in natural juice
Juice and rind 1 lime
2½ tbsps apricot brandy (optional)

1. Purée the apricots in their juice, using a liquidizer or food processor.

2. Put the apricot purée into a small saucepan.

3. Stir the lime juice and rind into the apricot mixture, and heat over a low temperature until it begins to boil.

4. Continue simmering over a low temperature until the sauce is thick and liquid has reduced.

Step 1 Purée the apricots in a liquidizer or food processor until they are smooth.

Step 3 Stir the lime juice and rind into the fruit purée, mixing well to blend evenly.

Step 4 Cook the apricot mixture over a low heat until the sauce has thickened and the liquid has evaporated.

5. Cool the purée in a refrigerator until required, and serve after stirring in the apricot brandy.

Cook's Notes

Time
Preparation takes 2 minutes, cooking takes 5 minutes.

Variation
Use canned pears or prunes in place of the apricots in this recipe.

Serving Idea
Serve with pancakes, or fresh fruit.

SERVES 10-12
APPLE SAUCE

This sauce is extremely versatile and can be used as an accompaniment to meats or fish, as well as being included in ingredients for desserts.

2lbs cooking apples
1¼ cups apple juice
⅓ tsp ground cloves
Finely pared rind ½ orange

1. Wash the apples and cut away any bruised or discolored pieces. Cut the fruit into large pieces.

2. Put the chopped fruit into a large pan, along with the apple juice, ground cloves and the orange rind. Bring to the boil and simmer until most of the liquid has evaporated and the fruit has softened.

3. Cool the cooked apples.

4. Put the cooled apples into a nylon sieve over a large bowl, and press through using the back of a wooden spoon, to remove all skin, pips and cores.

5. Put the apple purée into cartons or jars, and store or freeze until required.

6. Serve in a bowl and decorate with a sprig of mint.

Step 1 Wash the apples and cut away any bruising or discolored pieces.

Step 2 Cook the apples in the fruit juice until the liquid has reduced, and the fruit is soft and pulpy.

Step 4 Press the cooled fruit through a nylon sieve into a bowl, using the back of a wooden spoon to push the fruit purée through and to remove the cores, skin and pips.

Cook's Notes

Time
Preparation takes approximately 30 minutes, cooking takes about 20 minutes.

Preparation
If preferred, the cooked apples can be puréed in a liquidizer or food processor before pressing through the sieve to remove the skins and cores.

Variation
Use cinnamon instead of the cloves in this recipe.

Freezing
This sauce can be frozen for up to 4 months.

MAKES 10-12 PANCAKES
CREPES

These tasty pancakes are delicious with both sweet and tangy sauces.

1 cup all-purpose flour
Pinch salt
1 egg
1¼ cups milk
1¼ tsps vegetable oil
Juice and rind of a lemon and orange

1. Sieve the flour and the salt into a large bowl. Push the flour gently towards the sides of the bowl to make a well in the center.

2. Put the egg and the milk into a jug and beat well.

3. Gradually add the egg and milk mixture to the flour, pouring it into the center of the bowl, and mixing gently by stirring and drawing the flour in from the sides.

4. Continue adding the egg mixture gradually and beat until all the flour has been incorporated.

5. Heat a little oil in a small frying pan, and pour in enough batter to make a thin pancake.

6. Quickly tilt and rotate the frying pan so that the batter coats the bottom of it evenly.

7. Cook the pancake over a moderate heat until the underside has turned brown and the top has set.

8. Carefully turn the pancake over and brown the other side in the same way.

9. Turn each pancake out onto wax paper and keep them warm until required.

10. Serve the pancakes hot with freshly squeezed orange and lemon juice and decorate with the pared citrus rind.

Step 1 Gently push the flour towards the sides of the bowl to make a well in the center.

Step 3 Gradually add the egg and milk to the flour, mixing from the center of the bowl and drawing the flour into the liquid.

Step 6 Quickly tilt and rotate the frying pan so that the batter coats the bottom thinly.

Cook's Notes

Time
Preparation takes approximately 10 minutes, cooking takes about 20 minutes for all the pancakes.

Watchpoint
Do not overheat your frying pan or the base of the pancake will burn before the top has set. Also, do not attempt to turn the pancakes until the underside is properly cooked.

Freezing
Pancakes can be made in greater quantities than this recipe, and frozen until required.

MAKES 2 x 2 PINT PUDDINGS

PLUM PUDDING

Plum puddings are always thought of as being sweet and heavy. Try this sugar-free recipe for a fresh tasting change.

1lb mixed dried fruit
1 cup seedless raisins
1 cup pitted dates
1 cup pitted, ready to use prunes
½ cup blanched shredded almonds
3 cups fresh white breadcrumbs
⅔ cup shredded suet
1½ cups all-purpose flour
½ tsp ground nutmeg
¾ tsp ground cinnamon
¼ tsp salt
1 carrot, grated
1 cooking apple, grated
Grated rind and juice 1 orange
⅔ cup brandy, or stout
1 egg

1. Put all the fruit into a mincer or food processor and chop finely.

2. Put the chopped fruits into a large mixing bowl, add all the remaining ingredients, and mix well.

3. Grease 2 x 2 pint pudding bowls, and divide the mixture evenly between both bowls.

4. Cover the top of the puddings with a buttered circle of wax paper.

5. Make a foil pudding lid by cutting a large piece of aluminum foil, and pleating it down the center. Tie this lid securely onto the bowls.

6. Stand the puddings on an up-turned saucer or trivet, in a large saucepan.

7. Add enough boiling water to the saucepans to come two thirds of the way up the side of the pudding bowls.

8. Cover the saucepans and boil the puddings for 4-5 hours, keeping the water topped up as it evaporates.

9. Remove the bowls from the water and remove the covering paper.

10. Up-turn a serving plate over the puddings, and turn the whole pudding over, shaking it gently to help it drop out of the bowl onto the serving plate.

11. Serve ignited with brandy, if desired.

Step 2 Mix the minced fruit together in a large bowl with all the remaining ingredients, stirring well to blend thoroughly.

Step 5 Cover the pudding with a pleated foil pudding lid, tying this down securely before boiling.

Cook's Notes

Time
Preparation takes approximately 30 minutes, cooking takes about 5 hours.

Serving Idea
Serve with brandy butter or fresh cream.

Preparation
To be at its best this pudding should be prepared at least 3 months in advance.

Cook's Tip
This pudding can be stored for up to a year. To re-heat before use, pop into a pan of simmering water and cook for 3 hours.

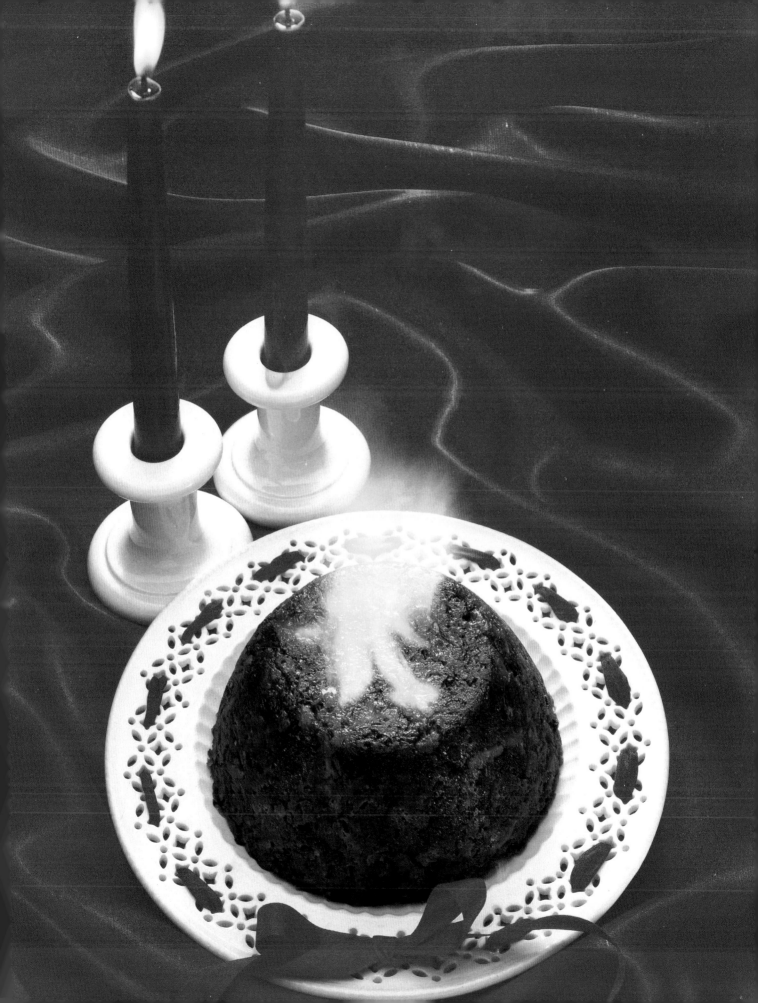

SERVES 4-6

COCONUT SORBET

Naturally sweet coconut milk and dark rum blend lusciously to produce a sorbet rich with the flavors of the Caribbean.

14oz can coconut milk
⅓ cup mineral water
⅓ cup dark rum
2 egg whites
Liquid sweetener to taste (optional)
2 bananas, thinly sliced and brushed with lemon juice and flaked coconut, to decorate

1. Mix the coconut milk with the mineral water, rum and liquid sweetener to taste, if required. Pour into a large freezer container and put into the freezer for 1 hour, or until the sides are beginning to freeze.

2. Using a fork, break the frozen coconut mixture up into a thin slush, making sure that there are no large ice crystals left in the mixture. Return to the freezer and continue freezing for a further hour.

3. Remove the coconut mixture from the freezer, and break up as before with a fork to make a thicker slush. Return the mixture to the freezer whilst you whisk the egg whites.

4. Whisk the egg whites until they form soft peaks.

5. Remove the partially frozen coconut mixture from the freezer and make sure that it can be easily stirred.

6. Carefully fold the egg whites into the coconut mixture, mixing lightly but thoroughly to blend evenly.

Step 2 Break the crystals away from the edge of the freezer dish using a fork, and mixing well to make a thin slush.

Step 6 Fold the softly whipped egg whites into the partially frozen slush, mixing lightly but thoroughly, to blend evenly.

7. Return the sorbet to the freezer and freeze until completely set.

8. To serve, remove the sorbet from the freezer 10 minutes before it is required and break it up with a fork into large ice crystals. Pile the crystals into serving dishes and decorate with the banana and the flakes of coconut.

Cook's Notes

Time
Preparation takes approximately 20 minutes, freezing takes 2-3 hours.

Variation
Use pineapple juice in place of the rum, and serve with pineapple pieces and coconut flakes.

Preparation
Make sure that the ice crystals are not too wet when you fold in the egg whites, otherwise the mixture will separate during freezing.

Cook's Tip
Make double quantities of this sorbet, as it freezes well for up to 3 months and is ideal as a stand-by dessert.

SERVES 4-6
EXOTIC FRUIT SALAD

Mangoes are exceptionally sweet when ripe, and give this lovely fruit salad a natural tangy sweetness.

3 ripe peaches
3 kiwi fruits
1 large star fruit
⅔ cup fresh strawberries
2 well-ripened mangoes, each weighing about 12oz
Juice of half a lime
1 cup redcurrants
Few strawberry leaves for decoration

Step 9 Press the mango purée through a wire sieve, using a wooden spoon to remove the pips and skins from the redcurrants.

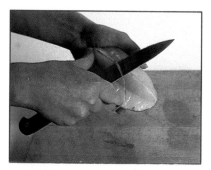

Step 5 Cut away any brown pieces from the skin of the star fruit using a sharp knife.

1. Plunge the peaches into boiling water for a few seconds, then carefully peel away the skin using a sharp knife.

2. Carefully cut the peaches in half and remove the stone.

3. Cut the peach halves into thin slices and arrange on a serving plate.

4. Cut away the peel from the kiwi fruits and slice them crosswise to show their attractive color.

5. Trim away any dark pieces from the skin of the star fruit, cut the flesh into thin slices, and remove any small pips you may find.

6. Leave the green stems on the strawberries and cut them in half lengthways. Arrange all the prepared fruit on the serving platter with the peaches.

7. Peel the mango and chop away the flesh from the large inner stone.

8. Put the chopped mango flesh into a liquidizer or food processor, along with the lime juice and half of the redcurrants.

9. Purée the mixture until smooth, then press the purée through a nylon sieve to remove the redcurrant skins and pips.

10. Sprinkle the remaining redcurrants over the fruit on the serving platter, removing any hard stems or leaves as you do so.

11. Pour the fruit purée evenly over the fruit salad, and chill for at least 1 hour before serving, decorated with the strawberry leaves.

Cook's Notes

 Time
Preparation takes approximately 25 minutes, plus 1 hour chilling time.

 Variation
Use any combination of your favorite fruits in the fruit salad, but do not change the mango purée.

 Preparation
If you do not have a liquidizer or food processor, a really ripe mango will rub easily through a wire sieve and will not need to be reduced to a purée first.

 Cook's Tip
Add 3 tbsps rum to the mango purée to give extra flavor for a special occasion.

SERVES 6

RASPBERRY SOUFFLÉ

This light dessert is the perfect finale for a dinner party.

1lb raspberries
Liquid sweetener to taste
2 tbsps gelatin
⅔ cup hot water
4 eggs, separated
1¼ cups heavy cream

1. Prepare a 6-inch souffle dish by tightly tying a lightly oiled sheet of wax paper carefully around the outside edge of the souffle dish, allowing it to stand approximately 4 inches above the rim of the dish.

2. Reserve a few of the raspberries for decoration, and purée the remainder using a liquidizer or food processor.

3. Rub the puréed raspberries through a nylon sieve to remove the hard pips.

4. Sweeten the smooth raspberry purée with the liquid sweetener and set aside.

5. Dissolve the gelatin in the hot water, stirring gently until it is completely dissolved and the liquid is clear.

6. Allow the gelatin to cool slightly and then beat it into the raspberry purée along with the egg yolks, mixing until all ingredients are well blended. Chill in the refrigerator until partially set.

7. Whisk the egg whites until they form soft peaks.

8. Lightly whip half of the heavy cream until it is softly stiff.

9. Remove the partially set raspberry mixture from the refrigerator, and carefully fold in the cream and the egg

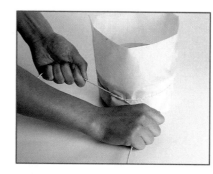

Step 1 Tie a sheet of wax paper around the souffle dish, to form a collar rising above the rim of the dish.

Step 3 Press the raspberry purée through a metal sieve, to remove the pips.

whites, blending lightly but thoroughly until the mixture is smooth.

10. Turn the prepared souffle mixture into the dish, allowing it to rise about 1 inch above the rim of the dish inside the paper collar. Allow to set in the refrigerator.

11. When completely set, remove the collar carefully and decorate the souffle with the remaining whipped cream and the reserved raspberries.

Cook's Notes

Time
Preparation takes approximately 40 minutes, plus chilling time.

Watchpoint
Do not add the gelatin to boiling water, or this will impair its setting qualities.

Preparation
Take great care not to over-mix the souffle mixture when adding the egg whites, or there will not be enough to rise up over the rim of the dish inside the collar.

Variation
Use strawberries, or any other favorite fresh fruit in place of the raspberries in this recipe.

Freezing
Cold souffles freeze very well for up to 6 weeks, but should be decorated after they have thawed.

SERVES 4
PASSION FRUIT ICE CREAM

Fruit ice creams are actually more refreshing without added sugar, but if you must have added sweetness use liquid sweetener.

6 passion fruits
1¼ cups natural yogurt
2 egg yolks
Liquid sweetener to taste (optional)
1-2 passion fruits, halved and scooped for decoration

Step 4 Break up the partially frozen passion fruit ice cream using a fork, and mixing until a smooth slush is formed.

Step 1 Cut the 6 passion fruits in half and scoop all the center pulp into a bowl using a small spoon.

Step 2 Beat together the yogurt, egg yolks and passion fruit pulp until they are well blended.

1. Halve the 6 passion fruits, and scoop out all the center pulp into a bowl.

2. Add the yogurt and egg yolks to the passion fruit pulp, and mix together well, adding liquid sweetener to taste, if desired.

3. Pour the passion fruit mixture into a shallow container, and freeze until partially set – approximately 1 hour.

4. Break the ice crystals in the partially set passion fruit mixture using a fork, and mixing well until they form a smooth slush.

5. Return the ice cream to the freezer and freeze until completely firm.

6. To serve, remove the ice cream from the freezer for 10 minutes, then pile scoops of ice cream into stemmed glasses, and serve with passion fruit pulp poured over each portion.

Cook's Notes

Time
Preparation takes approximately 20 minutes, plus freezing time.

Variation
Add 2 tbsps rum or brandy to the ice cream mixture before freezing.

Watchpoint
This ice cream goes extremely hard when frozen, so it is important to remember to remove it from the freezer 10 minutes before serving.

SERVES 4

STUFFED FIGS

Fresh figs are now easily available from most major supermarkets and good greengrocers. When ripe, they go a luscious purple black and are soft to the touch.

4 large ripe figs
5 tbsps ground almonds
2½ tbsps orange juice
2½ tbsps finely chopped dried apricots
5 tbsps natural yogurt
Finely grated rind ½ orange
Wedges of figs and mint, or strawberry leaves for
    decoration

Step 2 Ease the four sections of each fig outwards to form a flower shape.

Step 1 Carefully cut a cross into each fig, making sure that you do not cut right through the base.

Step 4 Divide the almond mixture evenly between the four figs, and press it into the center of each one.

1. Cut each fig into four quarters using a sharp knife, and taking care not to cut right down through the base.

2. Ease the four sections of each fig outward to form a flower shape.

3. Put the ground almonds, orange juice and chopped apricots into a small bowl and mix together thoroughly.

4. Divide this mixture into four, and press it into the center

of each fig.

5. For the sauce, mix the yogurt with the orange rind, and thin it down with just a little water, or orange juice.

6. Spoon a small pool of orange yogurt onto each of four plates, and sit a stuffed fig into the center of each pool. Decorate with the additional wedges of fig, and the mint or strawberry leaves.

Cook's Notes

Time
Preparation takes approximately 25 minutes.

Variation
Use peach halves instead of the figs in this recipe.

Watchpoint
Do not add too much water or orange juice to the sauce, or it will become too thin.

SERVES 6

CHERRIES IN SYRUP

Black cherries and apple juice combine perfectly in this tasty dessert.

1½lbs fresh black cherries
2 cups apple or grape juice
1¾ tsps finely grated lemon rind
3 tbsps cornstarch or arrowroot
3¾ tbsps brandy (optional)

1. Remove the stones from the cherries, using a cherry pitter or the rounded end of a potato peeler.

2. Put the pitted cherries into a saucepan, along with the apple or grape juice and the lemon rind. Bring to the boil over a moderate heat, then simmer for 10 minutes, or until the cherries are gently poached.

3. Remove the cherries from the juice with a slotted spoon, leaving the juice in the saucepan. Arrange the cherries in a serving bowl.

4. Blend the cornstarch with 5 tbsps of the cherry juice.

5. Add the blended cornstarch or arrowroot to the cherry juice in the pan, and bring to the boil stirring constantly until the sauce has thickened. Stir in the brandy if used.

6. Pour the thickened cherry sauce over the cherries in the bowl, and chill well before serving.

Step 1 Remove the stones from the cherries using a cherry pitter or the rounded end of a potato peeler.

Step 4 Blend cornstarch or arrowroot with 5 tbsps of the cherry juice.

Step 5 Bring the cherry juice and blended cornstarch or arrowroot, slowly to the boil, stirring all the time until the sauce thickens and clears.

Cook's Notes

Time
Preparation takes 15-20 minutes, cooking takes about 5 minutes plus chilling time.

Cook's Tip
Arrowroot will produce a clearer sauce than cornstarch.

Variation
Use apricots instead of cherries in this recipe.

Freezing
This recipe freezes well.

SERVES 4-6

ORANGE AND APRICOT MOUSSE

This delicious light mousse makes an ideal end to any meal.

2 oranges
3 x 14oz cans of apricots in natural juice, drained
Artificial sweetener to taste (optional)
2 tbsps powdered gelatin
⅔ cup natural yogurt
2 egg whites
Extra orange rind to decorate

1. Finely grate the rind from half of one orange using a fine grater.

2. Cut all the oranges in half and squeeze out the juice.

3. Put the drained apricots, all but 3 tbsps of the orange juice, and the orange rind into a liquidizer or food processor, and purée until smooth. Pour into a large bowl and set aside.

4. Put the 3 tbsps of orange juice into a small pan and heat gently, but do not boil.

5. Sprinkle the gelatin over the warm orange juice, and allow to stand until dissolved and clear.

6. Stir the gelatin mixture into the apricot purée, along with the natural yogurt, mixing well to blend evenly. Put in a refrigerator for about 30 minutes until almost set.

7. Whisk the egg whites until they form soft peaks.

8. Fold the whisked egg whites lightly, but thoroughly, into the partially set apricot mixture.

9. Divide the fruit mousse evenly into serving glasses and chill until completely set.

Step 3 Purée the orange juice, rind and apricots together in a liquidizer or food processor until smooth.

Step 6 Allow the fruit purée and gelatin to chill in a refrigerator until it is just beginning to set.

Step 8 Fold the egg whites carefully, but thoroughly, into the thickening fruit mixture, taking care not to over mix and lose the air in the egg whites.

Cook's Notes

Time
Preparation takes 30-35 minutes, plus chilling time.

Variation
Use strawberries or peaches in place of the apricots.

Serving Idea
Serve decorated with twisted strips of orange peel and a crisp biscuit if liked.

SERVES 6

BAKED APPLES IN PASTRY

Pastry sweetened with cinnamon and spices combines with a rich fruit filling to make this warming winter dessert.

3 cups all-purpose flour
¼ tsp salt
⅓ tsp cinnamon
⅓ tsp ground nutmeg
¾ cup butter
6-8 tbsps iced water
6 medium-sized dessert apples
6 prunes, pitted
6 dried apricots
2½ tbsps raisins
1 egg, beaten to glaze
Fresh cream to serve
Fresh mint to serve

1. Sift the flour, salt and spices into a large bowl.

2. Cut the butter into dice and rub into the flour until the mixture resembles fine breadcrumbs.

3. Mix in enough water to produce a smooth pliable dough.

4. Divide the dough into six pieces and roll out into a square approximately 8 inches.

5. Peel the apples with a sharp knife and carefully remove the center cores with an apple corer.

6. Chop the prunes and the apricots and mix these with the raisins.

Step 8 Draw the sides of the pastry square up and over each apple, sealing the edges well with a little water.

7. Place one prepared apple into the center of each pastry square, and fill the cavities with equal amounts of the dried fruit mixture.

8. Brush the edges of each square with a little water, and draw them up and around the sides of the apples, sealing them well with a little water and trimming off any excess pastry to give a neat finish.

9. Roll out the pastry trimmings, cut into decorative leaves and stick the leaves onto each apple for decoration.

10. Glaze each pastry apple with the beaten egg and place on a lightly greased cookie sheet.

11. Bake the apples in a preheated oven 350°F for 20-25 minutes, or until golden brown.

12. Serve hot with the fresh cream and sprigs of fresh mint.

Cook's Notes

Time
Preparation takes approximately 30 minutes, cooking time takes 20-25 minutes.

Cook's Tip
For an extra rich pastry, use 1 egg yolk and half the amount of water in this recipe.

Variation
Use pears instead of apples in this recipe.

Freezing
These apples freeze well after baking and should be thawed, then re-heated, before eating.

SERVES 6

ALMOND-YOGURT SHAKE

This healthy, sugar-free yogurt shake has a slightly salty, but refreshing flavor.

1¾ cups water
2 cups natural yogurt
2½ tsps lemon juice
2½ tbsps ground almonds
¼ tsp saffron strands
2½ tsps rose water
¼ tsp salt

1. Lightly moisten the rims of six tumblers with a little water or lightly whipped egg white. Spread a thin layer of salt onto a saucer and dip the moistened rims into it to coat lightly.

2. Put half of the water into a liquidizer and add the yogurt, lemon juice, almonds, saffron and rose water. Blend until smooth.

3. Mix in the remaining water and the salt.

4. Measure 1 pint of ice cubes into a measuring jug.

5. Pour the yogurt mixture from the liquidizer into another large jug.

6. Put half of the ice into the liquidizer and pour over half of the yogurt and saffron mixture. Blend to a thick slush, then repeat with the remaining ice and yogurt mixture. Serve in the prepared tumblers.

Step 2 Blend the water, yogurt, lemon juice, almonds, saffron and rose water in a liquidizer or food processor, until smooth.

Step 1 Lightly moisten the rims of six tumblers with a little water or lightly whipped egg white. Spread a thin layer of salt onto a saucer and dip the moistened rims into it to coat lightly.

Step 6 Blend half of the ice with half of the liquid in the liquidizer until it forms a smooth slush.

Cook's Notes

Time
Preparation takes 10 minutes.

Cook's Tip
If you haven't got a liquidizer or food processor, use a rolling pin to crush the ice.

Variation
Use the juice of ½ an orange in place of the lemon juice in this recipe.

SERVES 6

KIWI AND PINEAPPLE SHAKE

Sugar-free lemonade is easily available in supermarkets, and adds a tangy fizz to this delicious fruity drink.

1 cup pineapple juice
3 kiwi fruits
1¼ cups natural yogurt
1 lemon
Liquid sweetener to taste
2 cups ice cubes
1¼ cups sugar-free lemonade
1 kiwi fruit for decoration

Step 1 Purée the pineapple juice and kiwi fruits together in a liquidizer or food processor, until smooth.

1. Carefully peel the 3 kiwi fruits and roughly chop the flesh. Put the kiwi flesh into a food processor or liquidizer, along with the pineapple juice, and blend until smooth.

2. Finely grate the rind from half of the lemon and squeeze the juice. Mix the juice into the yogurt in a large jug, along with the fruit purée and liquid sweetener.

3. Put the ice cubes into the food processor or liquidizer, and pour over the pineapple and yogurt mixture. Blend for

15-30 seconds until it becomes a smooth slush.

4. Divide this mixture between six glasses and top up with lemonade, stirring well with a long handled spoon to blend in the glass.

5. Cut the unpeeled kiwi fruit into thin slices and slit each slice halfway through. Stand each slice of kiwi onto the sides of each glass for decoration.

Step 2 Blend the yogurt, lemon rind and juice, liquid sweetener, and the pineapple and kiwi fruit mixture together in a large jug.

Step 3 Blend together the ice and the pineapple yogurt mixture until it becomes a smooth slush.

Cook's Notes

Time
Preparation takes 5-10 minutes.

Cook's Tip
Do not use set yogurt in this drink as it will not blend smoothly.

Variation
Use orange juice in place of the pineapple juice in this recipe.

SERVES 4

TROPICAL FRUIT HEALTH DRINK

This healthful fruit drink is an ideal breakfast time treat.

3 kiwi fruits
2 ripe nectarines or peaches
2 slices fresh pineapple
1 lime
1¼ cups unsweetened pineapple juice
1 kiwi fruit or lime, for decoration

Step 2 Carefully peel away the skin from the blanched nectarines or peaches, using a sharp knife.

Step 3 Cut the peaches in half and twist them carefully apart to remove the stones.

Step 5 Blend the fruit and the juices in a liquidizer or food processor, until smooth.

1. Carefully remove the peel from the kiwi fruit and roughly chop the flesh.

2. Plunge the nectarines or peaches into boiling water for 30 seconds and carefully peel off the blanched skins.

3. Halve the peaches or nectarines, and remove the stones. Chop the flesh and put this into a liquidizer or food processor, along with the kiwi fruit.

4. Remove the peel from the pineapple slices and cut into quarters. Cut away the tough core from the pineapple and add the remaining flesh to the kiwi and peaches in the liquidizer or food processor.

5. Squeeze the juice from the lime and add this, with the pineapple juice, to the fruit in the food processor. Blend until smooth, and pour into individual serving glasses.

6. Decorate the edge of the glasses with thin slices of un-peeled kiwi fruit or lime.

Cook's Notes

Time
Preparation takes approximately 10 minutes.

Variation
Add 1¼ cups sugar-free lemonade to this recipe for a lighter more refreshing fruit drink.

Serving Idea
Serve spooned over muesli for a refreshing breakfast.

SERVES 4-6

SPICED MANGO JUICE

Fresh mango juice is not easily available in shops, but is so easy to make that it is well worth producing your own.

3 large ripe mangoes
⅔ tsp ground ginger
⅔ tsp ground cinnamon
1¼ cups unsweetened orange juice
1 lemon
1 orange for decoration

1. Peel the mangoes and cut the flesh away from the stone.

2. Put the mango flesh into a liquidizer or food processor along with the spices and orange juice. Blend until smooth.

3. Cut the lemon in half and squeeze the juice.

4. Add enough lemon juice to the mango purée to suit your own preference.

5. Pour the mango juice into individual serving glasses.

6. Slice the orange thinly and use these to decorate the sides of the glass.

Step 1 Carefully cut away the mango flesh from the long inside stone using a sharp knife.

Step 2 Blend the fruit, spices and orange juice together in a liquidizer or food processor, until they are smooth.

Cook's Notes

Time
Preparation takes about 15 minutes.

Cook's Tip
Use this drink, mixed with ½ cup dark rum for an unusual cocktail.

Variation
Add 1 large peeled banana to the mango mixture before puréeing for a thicker, and more filling breakfast drink.

SERVES 6-8

CARDAMOM-SPICED COFFEE

This rich spicy flavored coffee is a traditional drink in Arabian countries.

4½ cups water
1¾ cups milk
2½ tbsps fresh ground roast coffee
Seeds of 4 small cardamoms, crushed

Step 2 Add the coffee to the boiled water and milk, and mix well.

Step 3 Crush the cardamom seeds in a pestle and mortar until they are fine.

Step 4 Strain the coffee mixture through a metal sieve to remove the ground cardamom seeds.

1. Put the water and milk into a saucepan and bring to the boil.

2. Add the coffee and mix well.

3. Crush the cardamom seeds finely using a pestle and mortar. Stir into the coffee and liquid in the saucepan. Cover the pan and remove from the heat. Allow to stand for

2-3 minutes.

4. Strain the coffee mixture through a metal sieve into cups and serve straight away.

Cook's Notes

Time
Preparation takes about 8 minutes.

Cook's Tip
If you have a coffee grinder, grind the coffee beans yourself for a really fresh flavor.

Variation
Omit the cardamoms from this recipe if preferred.

SERVES 6

ORANGE-SPICED TEA

A deliciously different way of serving tea, this recipe is refreshing served either hot or cold.

4½ cups water
½-inch piece cinnamon stick
4 cloves
Seeds of 4 cardamoms
3 strips of orange peel
2½ tbsps tea leaves
Milk to taste

1. Put the cinnamon, cloves and cardamom seeds into a pestle and mortar and crush roughly.

2. Put the water into a large saucepan with the orange peel and bring to the boil.

3. Remove the saucepan from the heat and add the spices and tea leaves. Allow to infuse for 2-3 minutes, keeping the pan covered.

4. Strain the tea through a fine tea strainer into cups, and serve with milk if preferred, or black with a sprig of mint.

Step 2 Bring the water and orange peel to the boil.

Step 1 Crush the cinnamon, cloves and cardamom seeds roughly in a pestle and mortar.

Step 4 Strain the infused tea into cups through a fine tea strainer to remove the tea leaves and flavorings.

Cook's Notes

Time
Preparation takes 10-15 minutes.

SERVES 4

GRAPEFRUIT CUP

Ruby grapefruits give this delicious refreshing drink a lovely color as well as a natural sweetness.

2 ruby grapefruits
1¼ cups unsweetened grapefruit juice, preferably ruby
½ cup water
2 egg whites
Small sprigs of fresh mint to decorate

1. Carefully cut the peel from around the grapefruits, removing all the white pith as you go.

2. Cut the grapefruits into segments by carefully slicing between the flesh and the thin inner membranes.

3. Put the grapefruit segments, grapefruit juice, and the water into a liquidizer or food processor, and blend until smooth.

4. Add the egg whites to the grapefruit mixture and blend once again until it becomes frothy.

5. Pour the drink into glasses, making sure that a good portion of the white froth goes into each one.

6. Decorate with the sprigs of mint and serve immediately.

Step 1 Carefully cut away all the peel and the pith from each grapefruit, using a sharp knife.

Step 2 Cut the grapefruit segments away from the thin inner membranes using a sharp knife.

Cook's Notes

Time
Preparation takes 10-15 minutes.

Variation
Use normal grapefruits or sweet grapefruits for a variation in flavor.

Preparation
Squeeze all the juice from the discarded membrane into the liquidizer before blending.

Cook's Tip
For a speedy method of preparing this drink, use a can of unsweetened grapefruit segments in place of the fresh fruit in this recipe.

SERVES 4

GRAPEFRUIT CUP

Ruby grapefruits give this delicious refreshing drink a lovely color as well as a natural sweetness.

2 ruby grapefruits
1¼ cups unsweetened grapefruit juice, preferably ruby
½ cup water
2 egg whites
Small sprigs of fresh mint to decorate

1. Carefully cut the peel from around the grapefruits, removing all the white pith as you go.

2. Cut the grapefruits into segments by carefully slicing between the flesh and the thin inner membranes.

3. Put the grapefruit segments, grapefruit juice, and the water into a liquidizer or food processor, and blend until smooth.

4. Add the egg whites to the grapefruit mixture and blend once again until it becomes frothy.

5. Pour the drink into glasses, making sure that a good portion of the white froth goes into each one.

6. Decorate with the sprigs of mint and serve immediately.

Step 1 Carefully cut away all the peel and the pith from each grapefruit, using a sharp knife.

Step 2 Cut the grapefruit segments away from the thin inner membranes using a sharp knife.

Cook's Notes

Time
Preparation takes 10-15 minutes.

Variation
Use normal grapefruits or sweet grapefruits for a variation in flavor.

Preparation
Squeeze all the juice from the discarded membrane into the liquidizer before blending.

Cook's Tip
For a speedy method of preparing this drink, use a can of unsweetened grapefruit segments in place of the fresh fruit in this recipe.

INDEX